50

Fabulous

PARTIES

FOR KIDS

Also by Linda Hetzer

The Simple Art of Napkin Folding
Successful Entertaining
Illustrated Crafts series

50 Fabulous PARTIES FOR KIDS

LINDA HETZER

Illustrations by Meg Hartigan

CROWN TRADE PAPERBACKS / NEW YORK

To
Emily and Elizabeth
with love

Published by Crown Publishers, Inc., 201 East 50th Street,
New York, New York 10022. Member of the Crown Publishing Group.
Random House, Inc. New York, Toronto, London, Sydney, Auckland

CROWN TRADE PAPERBACKS and colophon are trademarks of Crown Publishers, Inc.
Manufactured in the United States of America

LIBRARY OF CONGRESS CATALOGING-IN-PUBLICATION DATA
Hetzer, Linda
50 fabulous parties for kids / by Linda Hetzer ; illustrated by Meg Hartigan. — 1st ed.
p. cm. Includes index.
1. Children's parties. I. Title. II. Title: Fifty fabulous parties for kids.
GV1205.H48 1994
793.2'1—dc20 93-5623
ISBN 0-517-88073-3

10 9 8 7 6 5 4 3 2

CONTENTS

~~~

PARTIES FOR CHILDREN AGES 10 TO 12

HOLIDAYS AND FAMILY EVENTS

ACKNOWLEDGMENTS

*M*any people help in what is the process of writing, of starting with an idea, and ending up with a book. I would like to thank the librarians in the Children's Room of the Epiphany branch of the New York Public Library for their invaluable assistance, and the wonderful people at City Harvest for so speedily picking up the cakes and distributing them to the needy. Thanks also to Rabbi Deborah Hirsch, Larry Kaplan, Faith Hamlin, and Irene Prokop for their contributions. And a special thank you to Michael Ginsburg for his love and support .

PLANNING PERFECT PARTIES

*I*magine you are a child and you can have any kind of party you want. Think of all the things you could celebrate—your birthday, family events, traditional holidays. What would you want to do?

As an adult, planning a party for a child can feel overwhelming. The thought of eight 7-year-olds looking up at you expectantly can cause even the most self-assured person a moment or two of sheer terror. But if you imagine you are a child again and ask the question "What do you want to do?" you have taken the first step to a successful party. And, most important, ask the question of the child for whom the party is planned, because a party will mean more to a child if he makes some of the decisions himself. When you include your child in the plans, you validate her and make her feel good about herself. And that's what a party is for, to have fun, to feel good about ourselves, and to celebrate life's events.

To help you answer the question of what to do, this book presents ideas for 50 parties for birthdays for children from age 3 through 12 as well as for traditional holidays and milestones in family life. Each party has a theme because, frankly, having a theme makes a party easier to plan and can also make it more fun for the guests. Each party has suggestions for an invitation, decorations, games or an arts-and-crafts project, and refreshments, and all the suggestions play a part in the theme.

So don't be intimidated and think that only professional party planners can produce a successful children's party. Let your imagination soar and you'll create a memorable party that gets accolades from children and adults alike.

Choosing a Theme

As you choose a theme for your child's party, think about what your child likes to do. Talk with your child about the party, work with his or her likes and dislikes. If your child is enamored with fire trucks even though most children that age love dinosaurs, a party built around the theme of fire trucks will please your child more than a dinosaur party. But do not pressure your child to participate too much; keep the party activities and the child's participation in the decisions commensurate with his or her age and abilities.

Think about your child's abilities. If your child has not yet developed good small motor coordination, it would be frustrating for him or her to have a party where you teach magic tricks. If your child is adept artistically you may want to choose a party where the children create an art project that they will take home with them.

Your child's personality can help define the party. If your child is energetic and not easily confined, you may want to plan an outdoor party with lots of relay races. If your child likes to learn new things, you may want to use this curiosity in planning party games that include intellectual stimulation and tests of skill. A party may consist of a relatively quiet crafts activity, be full of boisterous running games, or even include a combination of both.

Think about the ways in which your child socializes. Does your child like only children of the same sex? Would your child like to be entertained by an adult or is he or she comfortable with children only? Choose a party theme that incorporates the ways in which your child plays with his or her friends.

How old is your child? When planning a party for very young children, remember that toddlers have a short attention span so the activities need to be quick and the party kept short, 1 to 1½ hours at most.

Children ages 6 to 9 are very curious and love to try new things. They are capable of completing an arts-and-crafts project and following the rules of a game. Children this age need to be busy for the entire party, usually 1½ to 2 hours long.

Older children like to think of themselves as sophisticated and independent. A child between 10 and 12 should be involved in the planning of the party and will have a definite opinion on which games and activities to include. For all ages, make sure you have enough adult supervision and limit the party to a specific area of your house.

How many children do you invite? Eight is a manageable number of party guests, but each party is as individual as each child. If your child handles himself or herself best with only a few people around, you may want to invite only 2 or 3 friends and plan a party that will work well with a small number of guests. If your child thrives on social activity and wants to invite the entire class, you can create a party that will accommodate a large number of guests. Be practical, though. Don't invite more children than your house or yard can comfortably contain or more than you feel you can manage. An old adage says the number of guests should be equal to the child's age, so a 4-year-old would invite 4 guests and an 8-year-old, 8 guests. This formula does not always work, but it does emphasize the fact that the younger the birthday child, the fewer guests should be invited.

The party themes in this book were created to help you and your child have a successful party, to help you plan the party easily, and to help make lasting memories for your child. The parties are arranged by age to help you in planning, but the age groups should not restrict you. I know of a 5-year-old boy who had a sleepover party and a 10-year-old girl who had a party where the guests brought their own dolls (or teddy bears). And remember, not every party has to have a theme to be successful. You can create your own party by taking games from one party, an activity from another, the cake from yet another, and eliminating the decorations. Use the suggestions that are most useful to you and the ones that are appropriate for your child.

The Structure of a Party

To some parents the idea of entertaining 6 to 12 youngsters for up to 2 hours is quite daunting. To make it easier, you can think of the party as having 4 distinct parts: an opening activity, the entertainment, the refreshments, and a closing activity.

The opening activity is an icebreaker just as it is for an adult party. It is an activity that will capture the children's attention as soon as they walk in the door and make the transition from home to the party smooth and hassle-free. For very young children, ages 3 to 5, the opening activity could be having favorite toys such as building blocks or small trucks available in the living room or party room. A party for older children may begin by having the guests participate in making the decorations, such as creating the cave drawings for a dinosaur party. For a very simple opening activity, give the children crayons and construction paper and let them draw whatever they like.

The entertainment is the main part of the party and should keep the children busy but not be so structured that the children feel confined. Entertainment may be games or an art project or both. The entertainment may be provided by an outside person, such as a magician who performs magic tricks or an animal lover who shows pets.

You may need a transition between the entertainment and the refreshments. If the children have been playing boisterous games, plan a quiet one to help them settle down. If they have been working with art materials, you will need a cleanup time to clear the table and to get the children's hands washed.

Party refreshments can be as simple as cake and a beverage or they can be a complete meal. For children, the presentation of the cake and getting to help the birthday child blow out the candles is exciting but the food itself is often of little interest. Some children eat quickly, others won't eat at all. When planning the party, remember that having cake and a drink won't take much time, even when you allow time for singing "Happy Birthday" and blowing out the candles. Serving sandwiches or pizza will take a little longer, but not much. Some children not interested in food or in eating may want to get up from the table and go back to the games or crafts activity. You can ask all the guests to remain at the table even if they are not eating, or you can allow the guests to wander about, whichever you feel comfortable with.

The final activity is a way of saying the party is over. As you plan this event, think of something that will help make the transition away from the party and back to their own homes easier for the children. For young children, this may be simply handing out the party favors. It is best to wait to give out the favors until the children have their coats on and are ready to leave. For older children, the last activity can be one that puts closure on the party events, such as a game of finding the party bags or handing out medals after a party of Olympics-style games. Opening the gifts as a final activity has worked well at my children's parties, but others choose not to open gifts until the guests have left. Saving the gifts until later often works better with younger children.

Party Tips

Send or deliver written invitations. Children love to get mail, and busy parents like to have a record of the party information. All the invitations suggested here will fit in a standard envelope, either a small one (3⅛ x 6⅛ inches) or a legal size (4½ x 9½ inches). If you want to create your own invitations, start with an 8 x 8½-inch piece of construction paper and fold it in half to form a card that is 4 x 8½ inches. This card or any shape cut from it will fit in a legal-size envelope.

If you find the idea of making your own invitations overwhelming, purchase invitations at your local stationery store and save your creative energy for the party itself.

Get help. Ask a friend or neighbor to help out. Or ask one or two of the parents to stay. For young children, you can ask the mother or father of a child who has difficulty separating from its parent. The child will feel more comfortable with the parent around and the parent will probably enjoy lending a hand. Phone any adults ahead of time so they can make arrangements to stay at the party.

Consider hiring your teenage baby-sitter or a teenage neighbor and a friend. Be specific about the jobs you want them to do. You may want a helper to play the games with the children, to assist with a crafts activity, or to serve and clean up the food. Give them the jobs you least want to do so you are free to participate in the actvities you enjoy most.

Ask someone to take pictures. Children love to look at photographs (or videos) of themselves, and what better event to look at than their own birthday party. But it is impossible to be the party giver and to record the event. Before the day of the party, ask a friend or relative or another parent to take the pictures. Choose someone who is comfortable with a camera and who would enjoy doing it. Make sure the batteries are new and the flash is working, and buy several rolls of film.

You may want to take instant photographs of the children. Sometimes these become part of the party as, for example, when the children make a frame for their photograph. If the children come in costume or if they make a mask during the party, it is nice to include an instant photograph of each child in the bag of party favors.

If you have someone take pictures with a video camera, remember to be natural. Let the party happen and catch some of it on film. Don't plan each event so that it can be videotaped, because then the camera becomes intrusive and puts a damper on the fun.

Be prepared. Make all art projects yourself before the day of the party. Purchase the materials and make one sample of everything, whether it is a party hat you plan to make for the children or masks the children will make themselves. You need to know before the party what the finished artwork will look like, how much time it takes, and how easy or complex it is to make. All the materials used in the projects in this book are available in a variety store or stationery store. If you want to use different materials than the ones suggested, try them out. Have more material than you think you will need, in case there is a mishap and a child wants to start over.

Make sure you write each child's name on the back of each project he or she makes. You may think the children will remember their own artwork, but you don't want the end of the party disrupted by a fight over whose animal mask is whose.

Party favors or goody bags are standard fare at a party and all children expect to go home with something. What you give them will depend on the prevailing practice in your neighborhood, your budget, and what projects if any the children have made at the party. Be sparing with the candy because the children have just finished eating sweets. Flimsy dime-store favors often break before the party bag gets home, but elaborate goodies are not necessary either. Be inventive. Many of the parties described here include a list of favors that may help you choose what to put in your party bags.

Opening the gifts should be handled smoothly. Whether the birthday child opens the gifts during the party or when it is done will depend on your child's age and temperament and the structure of the party. Some parents whose children can't stand the suspense let them open each gift as the guest hands it to her or him. Other parents have the gift opening as the first activity. Both of these methods place too much emphasis on the gifts and not enough on socializing with friends. If the child thanks each guest for the gift as it is received, the gifts can be set aside (in another room if necessary) for later. If the gifts are opened as the closing event of the party, the birthday child can thank each guest individually and the guests will be able to see all the gifts.

When would a child not open the gifts at the party? If the children are very involved with the games or absorbed in an art project, time may run out before the gifts are opened. Many younger guests do not care about seeing their gift opened and would rather continue to play. If you have a very large party where an entire class of 20 or more is invited, it may be too unwieldy to have the birthday child unwrap that many gifts. It may be best in these circumstances to have the birthday child open the gifts with the family after the guests have left.

Writing thank-you notes is good social etiquette, and children should be encouraged to do it. Children can be introduced to the idea in stages that are appropriate for their age. Parents of a young child can write the note and have the child print the first letter in his or her name at the bottom of the note. As they get a little older, children can dictate the note to a parent and then write their name. Older children can and should write the notes themselves.

Some parents write or have the child write a generic thank-you note, photocopy it, and put a copy in the goody bag. This practice, while time-saving, does not establish the relationship between receiving a gift and writing a thank-you note and does not acknowledge the individual gift. A much more satisfactory solution would be a one-sentence thank-you note written by the child after the party.

Remember that thank-you notes are absolutely necessary if the gifts were not opened at the party.

The Party Cakes

Anyone can create the cakes in this book; you do not have to be artistic to make them. The cakes are quite easy and quick to do. If you love to be creative, the detailed instructions and careful line drawings will take you through the steps necessary to make these interestingly shaped cakes. For your convenience, the ingredients have been listed as follows: (1) all food items; (2) stationery items, such as construction paper and cardboard; (3) household items, such as glue and wax paper; and (4) tools, such as scissors and compass.

Everything you need to make these cakes can be purchased in your local supermarket. For the cakes, you can use an 18¼-ounce 2-layer cake mix, make your own favorite recipe, or buy a ready-made cake. If you use a cake mix, you can make the low-fat version (made without oil); the light cake will hold its shape even when it is cut into pieces. All the shapes in the book start with the most common cake pan sizes. You do not have to puchase any special cake pans.

For the frosting, you can buy a 16-ounce can of prepared frosting or you can make your own. When you use a can of prepared frosting, add 1 teaspoon of liquid such as vanilla or almond flavoring, food coloring, or water to thin the consistency a little and make it easier to apply to the cake. Always use regular frosting—the calories are worth it—because the low-fat variety has a stickier consistency and is not as easy to spread.

The decorations used include cake decorating gel and sprinkles, available in the baking aisle of your grocery store; candy such as gumdrops, licorice shoelaces, and candy corn; and cookies such as chocolate sandwich cookies and vanilla wafers.

For the best results, always allow the cake to cool completely before you cut it. Level the cake if the directions so indicate by cutting off the rounded top of the cake layer with a serrated knife. Do this while the cake is still in the pan. Also use a serrated knife to cut the cake into shapes, after first marking the areas to be cut with toothpicks.

When you frost the cake, drop teaspoons of frosting a couple of inches apart on the surface you are working on. Then use a spatula to smooth the frosting together. That way, the spatula will touch the frosting only and not the top of the cake so you will be less likely to get cake crumbs mixed in with the frosting. To make a straight line in the frosting, use a piece of dental floss held taut between your hands.

PARTIES

for

Children

AGES

3 TO 5

The Teddy Bears' Tea Party

Merry Music Makers

Be an Artist

A Circus Party

Fire Fighters' Parade

A Zoo Party

A Fairy-Tale Party

A Puppet Show

School Is In

A Picnic Party

THE TEDDY BEARS' TEA PARTY

*M*any young children bring their teddy bears wherever they go. What could be nicer for them than to receive a birthday party invitation that includes the teddy bear?

For a Teddy Bears' Tea Party you can decorate the party room with your child's collection of teddy bears. Borrow stuffed bears from friends and cousins to fill the room. At the party the children can make matching party hats and macaroni necklaces for themselves and for their bear.

The party will include lunch. You can set the table with the plastic plates and cups of a child's tea set, making a place setting for each child and each teddy bear. Make place cards for each place setting, one with the child's name and one with the teddy bear's name. To make the place cards, fold a 3 x 5-inch unlined index card in half and glue a miniature teddy bear cookie to the left side. To make teddy bear sandwiches, prepare your child's favorite sandwich on white bread and then cut them with a teddy bear cookie cutter. Serve apple juice in the teacups and have the big chocolate Teddy Bear Cake as the centerpiece of the lunch table.

For party favors you can give each child a paperback copy of a favorite teddy bear book. Such favorites around my house are *Corduroy* and *Corduroy's Pocket* by Don Freeman and *Mooncake* by Frank Asch. You can give each teddy bear a small box of miniature teddy bear cookies.

The Invitation

What you need:
Yellow construction paper
Teddy bear cookie cutter
Felt-tipped markers
Scissors

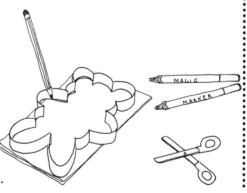

Holding a piece of construction paper horizontally, fold it into thirds accordion-style.

Trace the teddy bear cookie cutter onto the paper, making sure the arms extend to the folds of the paper. Keeping the paper folded, cut out the bear. Draw eyes, nose, mouth, ears, bow, and buttons with markers, then color in the fur with a brown marker. Open the bear and write the party information inside, inviting the child's teddy bear as well as the child. Ask for the teddy bear's name when the parents respond to the invitation so you can make place cards for the child and the teddy bear.

Matching Party Hats

What you need:
Construction paper, 12 x 18 inches
Small designs cut from
  leftover wrapping paper
Crayons
Glue stick
Clear tape
Needle and elastic thread or elastic cord
Pencil-and-string compass
Scissors

Using a piece of string tied to a pencil, draw and cut out a half-circle of construction paper with an 8-inch radius for the child's hat and a half-circle with a 4½-inch radius for the teddy bear's hat. Have the children decorate the hats by gluing on designs cut from wrapping paper and adding details with crayon. When the decorations are complete, roll the half-circles into a cone shape and secure the seam with clear tape. Thread the needle with an 8-inch length of elastic thread, sew through the hat on either side, and knot the thread ends. For the teddy bears' hats, adjust the length of elastic thread according to the size of the bear.

Macaroni and Bead Necklaces

What you need:
Yarn or string
Macaroni with hollow centers
Colorful wooden beads with large holes
Scissors
Tape measure

Cut a 26-inch length of yarn or string for each child and a smaller one for each teddy bear. (Loop a tape measure around the teddy bear to see what length yarn you need.) Have the children arrange the macaroni and beads on the table first, then string them on the yarn. Tie the ends of yarn together.

The Teddy Bear Cake

What you need:
1 cake mix
1 can chocolate frosting
1 tube white decorating icing
1 cup miniature chocolate chips
Candy: 2 licorice disks, 1 licorice shoelace, 3 gumdrops
Cake pans: one 8-inch round, one 8-inch square, one cupcake pan
Construction paper
Toothpicks

Mix the cake according to the package directions and divide the batter into the round pan, the square pan, and 4 cupcakes, filling 3 of the cupcakes barely half full and the fourth one more than three-quarters full. Bake the layers following package directions and allow to cool. Level the tops of the cakes with a serrated-edge knife.

Cut out the arm and leg pieces from the square cake. Cut off the

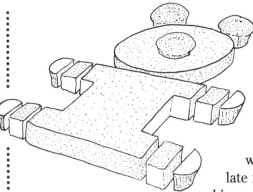

rounded top of the fourth cupcake and cut 2 cupcakes in half. Arrange the cake pieces as shown, placing the cupcake top in the center of the round cake for the teddy bear's nose. Level the cupcake halves.

Frost the entire teddy bear with chocolate frosting. To simulate fur, place miniature chocolate chips around the outside edge. For eyes, make a large circle with the white decorating icing, place a licorice disk in the center, and top with a drop of white icing. Make light chocolate frosting by mixing white icing with chocolate frosting, and frost the inside of the ears and paws. Place the rest of this frosting in a pastry bag and draw the nose and mouth. Tie a licorice shoelace in a bow and place under the chin. Use gumdrops for buttons. Write birthday greetings on a small piece of construction paper and glue to a toothpick. Insert in the teddy bear's paw.

Tips

✔Make your own pastry bag by cutting off the tip of one corner or a small plastic sandwich bag.

✔With a cake shape that has many cut edges like the Teddy Bear Cake, use a cake and frosting of the same color for a neater look. That way, any cake crumbs that may mix with the frosting do not mar the design.

✔If your child does not like chocolate, make a yellow cake with vanilla frosting and apply chocolate sprinkles for the fur.

✔To simulate fur, try using: chocolate sprinkles, chocolate curls shaved from a chocolate candy bar with a vegetable peeler, chopped nuts, coconut that has been tinted brown, miniature chocolate chips, or chocolate cookie crumbs.

MERRY MUSIC MAKERS

*Y*oung children love music and most of them are uninhibited enough to sing and play an instrument to their heart's content. A party with music as a theme will lead to clamorous good fun.

To decorate the room, cut out musical notes from black construction paper and hang them on the wall. You can also blow up balloons and decorate them with a musical note drawn with a black felt-tipped marker.

At the party, the children can make two musical instruments, a kazoo and maracas, and then play and sing their favorite songs. If the party is for very young children, 3-year-olds, you may want to make the maracas ahead of time and just have the children decorate them. If you decide to do this, remember to leave 1 maraca open so the children can see how it is made.

When the instruments are completed, you can lead the children in singing and playing favorite songs such as "Old Macdonald Had a Farm," "London Bridge," and "Twinkle Twinkle Little Star." They can also play games such as Musical Chairs or the other games described that use music.

And as you bring out the grand finale of the party, the Drum Cake, the children can play their maracas as they sing "Happy Birthday" to the birthday child.

The Invitation

What you need:
White and black
   construction paper
Felt-tipped marker
Glue
Scissors

Cut a 6 x 7-inch piece of white construction paper and fold it in half so you have a 3½ x 6-inch invitation. Draw a musical note on black paper, cut it out, and glue it to the invitation. With a marker, write "A note . . ." on the front and "to invite you to Jennifer's Musical Party" on the inside. Add the party information on the inside. This invitation will fit in a small commercial envelope for mailing.

Maracas

What you need:
An empty margarine tub with its cover for each maraca
⅓ cup uncooked rice or dried peas for each maraca
Pictures cut from magazines, shapes cut from construction paper, and children's stickers
5 inches of ½-inch-wide elastic for each maraca
Glue
Stapler

Attach the elastic to the top of the margarine tub cover by turning the ends of elastic in toward the center. Put several staples in each end of elastic to hold it. Fill the tub halfway with rice or peas. Put glue around the inside rim of the cover and put the cover on the tub. The glue can dry while you decorate the outside of the tub with magazine pictures, paper shapes, and stickers. Allow the glue to continue drying while you make the kazoos.

Kazoo

What you need:
Paper towel tube for each kazoo
5-inch square of wax paper for each kazoo
Rubber bands
Construction paper in a variety of colors
Stickers (optional)
Clear tape
Scissors

Cut the construction paper into 6 x 11-inch rectangles. Roll a piece of construction paper around each paper towel tube and secure with tape. The children can decorate the kazoo with stickers if they like. Cover one end of the tube with a wax paper square and hold it in place with a rubber band. To play the kazoo, hum into the open end of the tube.

Games

Musical Squares This game is a variation of Musical Chairs that does not require chairs. Tape sheets of colored construction paper on the floor, 1 sheet less than there are children at the party. As you play music the children walk around. When the music stops, each child must stand on a colored square. The child without a square is out. Remove 1 square and continue playing until only 1 player is left.

Musical Circles Have the children sit in 2 circles. Pass a ball around each circle. When the music stops, the children with the balls get up and change circles.

Musical Dance Have the children make 2 circles, one inside the other. Half the children will play maracas and half kazoos. As you play music have the children in each circle walk in opposite directions. When you stop the music, each child looks at the child opposite him. If they are both playing the same instrument, they drop out of the circle. Continue playing until all children have been matched up.

Drum Cake

What you need:
1 cake mix
1 can vanilla frosting
2 tubes decorating icing in contrasting colors
1 tube decorating gel
Decorating tips for use with a tube
   of decorating icing (optional)
Three 8-inch round cake pans
1 piece construction paper
Clear tape
Pencil
Toothpicks

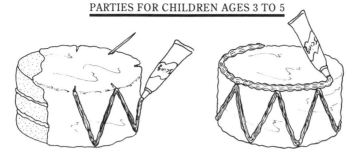

Mix the cake following package directions and bake it in the 3 round pans. Bake them for 5 minutes less than the suggested baking time for two layers. When the cake is cool, put frosting between each of the layers and then frost the entire shape. With a toothpick, make 8 marks evenly spaced around the top of the cake. With 1 color of decorating icing, draw diagonal lines from the marks on top to the bottom around the sides of the cake. With the contrasting color icing, draw 1 line around the bottom edge of the cake and a second line around the cake at the top edge, using a decorative tip on the decorating tube if you like.

To make the drumsticks, roll the construction paper around the pencil to curl it. It's easier to work with if you curl the paper first, then cut it. Cut two 11 x 2-inch strips from the paper. Roll one strip around the pencil to create a thin tube and secure it with clear tape; slip the pencil out. (The pencil is used to make the shape only.) Repeat for the second drumstick. Place the drumsticks on the top of the cake. With decorating gel, write "Happy Birthday Jennifer" on the cake.

Tips

✔ For an easy way to grease the cake pans, slip a plastic sandwich bag over your hand and spread about 1 tablespoon of butter or margarine in each pan.

✔ To smooth the top and sides of a frosted cake before you add decorations, use the edge of a piece of cardboard to wipe across the surface.

✔ When decorating the sides of a cake, use decorating icing instead of decorating gel. The gel is thinner and will slide off if the cake is decorated several hours ahead of time. The decorating icing will adhere to the cake frosting and will stay in place.

BE AN ARTIST

*a*rtwork created by young children is a joy to look at and what could be more fun for budding artists than to have a party where they can draw and color a self-portrait. At this party the children will make a life-size drawing of themselves and help create a drawing of a funny-looking person. You can take an instant photograph of each child and his or her finished drawing and put it in the child's bag of party favors. When all the artwork is completed you can serve the giant-size Crayon Cake.

For party favors, you can make a child's artist's kit containing several of the following supplies: a box of crayons, a set of watercolor paints, a coloring book, pencils, a large eraser, and drawing paper. Put these items in paper bags decorated with pencil, crayon, and paintbrush stickers and number the bags. Before the party begins, blow up balloons and put a numbered piece of paper inside each balloon. As the closing activity, the children can choose a balloon and break it. They receive the party bag that corresponds to the number in their balloon. The children will also take home their life-size drawings.

The Invitation

What you need:
Black or dark blue construction paper,
    8 x 8½ inches
Scraps of colored construction paper
White typing paper
Black felt-tipped marker
Glue
Scissors

Fold the black construction paper in half lengthwise. For the crayons, cut 4 x ¾-inch rectangles from the colored construction paper, and cut a point at one end. With black marker, draw stripes and an oval on the rectangles to make them look like crayon wrappers. Glue the crayons to the front of the invitation. Write the party information on a 3½ x 6-inch piece of typing paper and glue it to the inside of the invitation.

Life-Size Drawings

What you need:
Brown wrapping paper
Crayons or felt-tipped markers
Scissors

Place the brown wrapping paper on the floor. Ask each child in turn to lie down while you trace around them. Have each child color in their own drawing, encouraging them to be creative, even outlandish, with their clothing and accessories. When they have all finished, cut out the drawings and take an instant photograph of each child with his drawing.

Let's Make a Person

What you need:
White typing paper or construction paper
Crayons or markers
Clear tape

Give each child a piece of paper and assign them a part of the body. Depending on the number of children you have, you can assign the eyes, nose, and mouth to different children or give one child the face to draw and another one the hair. Assign the legs separately or give one child the legs and another the feet. You can draw the body or ask a child to do it, then tape the body parts in their appropriate places on the drawing. Hang up the result and have the children choose a name for the wonderful creature they have created.

Crayon Cake

What you need:
1 cake mix
1 can frosting
Food coloring
1 tube decorating gel
One 9 x 13-inch cake pan
Toothpicks

Bake the cake following package directions. When the cake is cool, cut it in half lengthwise. Level each half. Frost the top of one half and place the other half on top of the first one. Cut a point at one end of the cake.

You will need frosting in 2 shades of 1 color. Add food coloring to tint the frosting a pale color and frost the entire shape. Then add more food coloring to the remaining frosting until it is a considerably darker shade. With the darker frosting, frost the point and 1 inch of the top of the cake, and the bottom of the crayon and 1 inch of the top at the other end of the cake. With a toothpick, draw an oval in the center of the cake and draw two lines at each end of the lighter frosting so it looks like a crayon wrapper. Go over all the lines with decorating gel and write the birthday greetings in the center of the oval.

Tips

✔ If the cake is too large to fit on a plate or tray, make your own serving tray by covering a piece of cardboard with aluminum foil. When you finish decorating the cake, you can add paper doilies, flowers, or other accouterments around the edge of the cardboard to decorate the tray.

✔ When you make a design on a cake, such as drawing the oval in the center of the crayon, first draw the design with a toothpick. You can change the line if you want. Then, when you are satisfied with the line, you can draw over it with decorating gel.

✔ The shaded portions of the cake diagram are the parts of the cake that are not necessary for the design. You can crumble these up and serve them as a topping on ice cream, or you can offer them as treats to any children, big or small, who are helping you make the cake.

A CIRCUS PARTY

*a*t this Circus Party the children can dress up and pretend to be their favorite circus performer. To make a circus tent in the party room, attach crepe paper streamers to the center of the ceiling. Twist each streamer around itself and attach just below the top of the wall, letting the end hang halfway down the wall.

For the costumes, gather together old clothing and accessories. You will need enough so that the children can wear several different items. Encourage the children to sort through the boxes of clothes to create an outfit. You may want to have serveral adults or teenagers on hand to make suggestions and help the children get dressed. Allow plenty of time for the children to try on clothes and experiment. As each child is dressed, have someone paint their face and then take an instant photograph of her or him. When everyone is ready, start the games. Don't be surprised if some children are more interested in dressing up than in playing games and may choose to stay with the clothing.

For refreshments, serve the wonderful Clown Cupcakes with fruit juice. For party favors, give each child a box of CrackerJack and colorful items like modeling clay, colored shoelaces, and fancy stickers.

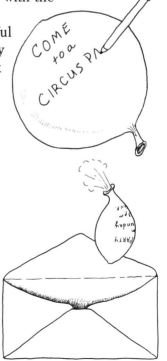

The Invitation

What you need:
10-inch or larger balloons
Felt-tipped marker or ballpoint pen

Have the marker open and ready to use. Blow up a balloon and while holding it in one hand write the party information on the inflated balloon with the marker. Let the ink dry for a few seconds, then deflate the balloon and put it in an envelope to mail. The ink in some markers does not dry well on a balloon, so use 1 balloon as a sample and try 1 or more markers or a ballpoint pen to see which ink works best on your balloons.

Costumes

Have 4 cardboard cartons, 2 for clothes, 1 each for shoes and headgear. Use your own clothes, older siblings' clothing, leftover Halloween costumes, household items like doilies and bathroom rugs, and any items you can pick up at a secondhand store or yard sale. Gather hats, wigs, scarves, and costume jewelry and put them in the box of headgear; for the shoe box include sneakers, sandals, plastic beach shoes, fuzzy bedroom slippers, and men's and women's dress shoes. You'll also want to have some of the following:

•Leotards, tights, and tutus for a bareback rider, tightrope walker, or acrobat.

•A suit jacket for the master of ceremonies or the lion tamer.

•A large T-shirt with sleeves stuffed with tissue paper for the strongman.

•A yellow or orange bathroom rug pinned to the back of a shirt for a lion, a gray sweatsuit for an elephant, and a brown bath towel for a horse.

•And for the clowns, the louder and more outrageous the colors and the bigger the clothing the better. Try to collect brightly patterned teenager's shorts, men's shirts with a loud print, brightly colored ties, out-of-style hats, colored knee socks, flowered dresses, plaid skirts, and striped blouses.

Games

May We Join the Circus? One child is the circus manager and all the other children line up opposite. The children ask, "May we join the circus?" and the manager replies, "Only if you're wearing green." Those children wearing green join the manager. Other responses could be "Only if you have blue eyes," "Only if you are wearing a skirt," "Only if you have circles (or dots) on your clothes," and so forth. When all the players join, then another player becomes the circus manager.

Ha Ha The object of this game is to laugh only as many times as your place in line. One child lies down on the floor, the next child lies down with his head on the first child's lap, the third child puts his head on the second child's lap. Continue this way until all the children are lying down. The first child says, "Ha," the second child says, "Ha, Ha," the third child says "Ha, Ha, Ha," and so on down the line. When a child dissolves in giggles, which happens often, that child is out. Continue playing to see who can keep from laughing.

Acrobats and Animals This game is a variation on Fruit Basket Upset. The children all sit in a circle. Assign a category to each child according to how he or she is dressed. Categories might include acrobats, bareback riders, tightrope walkers, animals, and clowns. One child without a seat calls out a category such as animals. All the animals get up and switch seats while the first child tries to find a space to sit. The child who doesn't find a seat is It and calls out the next category. When a child calls "Circus Upset," all of the children must get up and change seats.

The Magic Circle The children sit in a circle. The child who is It leaves the room while 2 children get up and change places. The child who is It tries to guess who changed places. If he is right, he sits down and someone else becomes It.

Clown Cupcakes

What you need:
1 cake mix
1 can vanilla frosting
1 tube decorating icing
1 tube each red and white decorating gel
M&M's
Gumdrops (optional)
Multicolored sprinkles and
    nonpareils
Ice-cream cones
Cupcake pans
Paper cupcake liners

Bake the cupcakes following package directions but fill the cupcake liners only half full. Allow the cupcakes to cool. You will have 30 cupcakes with which you can make 15 clowns.

Make the ice-cream cone hats while the cupcakes are cooling. For the 3-button hats, put 3 circles of decorating icing (not gel) on the cone and press an M&M into each circle. For the trimmed hats, put decorating icing around the rim of the cone and make 2 circles on the cone. Dip the icing-covered areas into sprinkles or nonpareils. To make the eyes with crosses, make an X with white decorating gel (not icing) on 2 M&M's and set them aside.

When the cupcakes are cool, remove the paper liners from half the cupcakes. Frost the top of a cupcake in a liner, place a plain cupcake upside down on top of it, and frost the top and sides of the plain cupcake. Place the cone hat on top of the frosted cupcake. Put M&M's in the frosting for the eyes and nose. For a larger nose, cut off the top of a gumdrop and place it on the cupcake. Draw a mouth with red decorating gel.

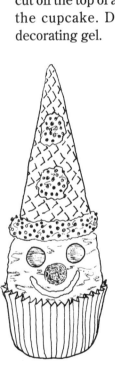

Tips

✔When making the Clown Cupcakes, frost a cupcake and then decorate the face right away rather than frosting all the cupcakes and then decorating them, because candy and sprinkles adhere better to fresh frosting that has not had a chance to dry slightly.

✔For the clown's facial features, try a variety of candy such as candy corn, Lifesavers, or chocolate chips, as well as chopped nuts and coconut to create different facial expressions.

FIRE FIGHTERS' PARADE

*M*any young children are fascinated by fire trucks and love to wave at the fire fighters as the trucks go by. For an exciting party for would-be fire fighters, take the children on a tour of your local firehouse so they can climb aboard a fire truck and see up close all the fire fighters' gear. When they return to your house for refreshments they will talk of nothing but the thrill of being on a real fire truck. And to add to this thrill is a Fire Truck Cake in the center of your party table.

The children can make their own Fire Fighter's Hat while you set up lunch of pizza and soda. Or you can make the hats before the party begins. The children will take home their hat and a prize they catch during the fishing game. You could also give them a small bag of several types of red candy like red hots, cherry Lifesavers, and cinnamon gum.

If a tour of the firehouse cannot be arranged, you can ask a local fire fighter to come to your house to display his clothing and equipment.

The Invitation

What you need:
Red and white construction paper
Black felt-tipped marker
Glue stick
Pencil
Scissors

Hold the red construction paper horizontally and draw a line from the top right corner to a point 3 inches up from the bottom left corner. Cut away the top area and fold the card into thirds and open it again (see next page).

From the white paper cut ¼-inch-wide strips: four 7-inch, two 5-inch, and twenty ¾-inch strips. To form the ladder, glue two 7-inch strips along the top edge, overlapping the strips slightly; glue the other two 7-inch strips ½-inch down from the first 2. Trim

the edges of the strips if they extend beyond the card. For the rungs, glue fifteen ¾-inch strips along the ladder, putting 5 strips on each third of the card. Turn the card over and glue the 5-inch strips to the center third of the card, then add the remaining 5 rungs. On the front of the card write "Climb the Fire Fighter's Ladder" and then open the card and write "To a party for Catherine" and give the party information.

Fire Fighter's Hat

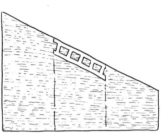

What you need:
Red construction paper
Pencil
Scissors
Black felt-tipped marker

Fold the construction paper in half lengthwise and draw the area to be cut out following the measurements on the diagram. Cut out the inner area and round off the front and back corners. Open up the construction paper and fold up the shield so it stands up straight. With marker, outline the shield and write the child's age or favorite number in the center. If you need to make the space for the head larger, fold the hat again and make the cut a little deeper.

Games

Pin the Pepperoni on the Pizza Cut a 30-inch circle from brown wrapping paper and draw a pizza crust around the edge. Color the center of the circle with red crayon. For pepperoni slices, cut 2-inch circles from brown wrapping paper and put a folded piece of clear tape on the back of each one. Blindfold each child in turn and have them pin a pepperoni slice on the pizza. Give a prize to the child whose pepperoni slice is closest to the center.

Rescue Divide the children into 2 teams. Give each team a kitchen spatula and a group of small plastic figures, about 1 to 2 inches in size. Place 2 cartons, 1 opposite each team. A child must carry a small figure on the spatula, place it in the carton, and run back to give the spatula to the next child. The first team that "rescues" all the people wins.

Fire Fighters' Parade Have the children sit in a circle with their eyes closed. One child is the first fire fighter. She walks around the circle quietly and taps a child on the shoulder. That child gets up without talking and follows the leader, who walks around the circle and taps the next child. When all the children have joined the line, have the leader take the parade to the table for refreshments.

Going Fishing Make a fishing pole by tying a string onto a stick. Tie a magnet on the end of the string. Wrap and tie small favors—a small red fire truck would be great. Attach a paper clip to the wrapped favor. When the children fish, the magnet will attach to the paper clip and catch a favor. Keep the toys small so the magnet can pick them up. You can play this game at the end of the party so the children are ready to leave when they have caught their prize.

Fire Truck Cake

What you need:
2 pound cakes
1 can vanilla frosting
Red food coloring
1 tube white decorating icing
4 chocolate sandwich cookies
2 licorice shoelaces, 2 white Lifesavers, 2 silver dragées

Level 1 pound cake. Cut out the top of the second one, as shown. Frost the top of the first pound cake and put the second one on top. Add red food coloring to the frosting and frost the entire shape. Place 2 sandwich cookies on each side for wheels. Cut pieces of licorice shoelace for the fenders. Put 2 Lifesavers in front for the headlights. With white decorating icing fill the inside of each candy and put a silver dragée in the center. With decorating icing make a rectangle on the front and sides for windows, draw a ladder on each side, and add spokes to the wheels. Cut pieces of licorice shoelace to outline each window.

Tips

✔To minimize the loose crumbs along the cut edges of a cake, you can cover these surfaces with jelly. Melt 2 to 3 teaspoons of jelly in a small saucepan and apply it to the cut surfaces with a pastry brush.

✔To make red frosting for the Fire Truck Cake requires a lot of red food coloring. Begin by adding several drops of food coloring and mixing it thoroughly. Continue adding the food coloring slowly and mixing it thoroughly until you are satisfied with the color.

A ZOO PARTY

a young child who loves animals will be thrilled to have a zoo created in her home for her next birthday party. For entertainment you can hire an animal trainer from your local zoo to show the children live zoo animals. Or you can ask a neighborhood animal lover to show pets such as a cat, guinea pig, hamster, ferret, turtle, or birds to the children. Remember to ask the trainer or animal lover which animals he or she plans to bring along. You may not want a snake, or any other animal that may upset children, at your party.

To decorate the room, place your child's collection of stuffed animals around the party room. If you need more animals, borrow some from family and friends. You want the room to look full. The children can make animal face masks while they are waiting for the animal trainer and play some animal games before you serve refreshments.

For favors you could give each child 1 item that has an animal theme, such as a mug in the shape of an animal's head, a coloring book of animals, or a T-shirt with an animal on the front. Or you could fill a goody bag with an assortment of candy and miniature animal toys. The children will also take home their masks. To complete the party, you can serve the Happy Lion Cake and milk to the hungry animal lovers.

The Invitation

What you need:
Construction paper
Coloring book with pictures of animals
Felt-tipped marker
Glue
Scissors

Cut out the pages of the coloring book and glue each one onto a piece of construction paper. Turn the paper over, fold it in thirds and write the party information on it with a marker. Tell the children they may color in the drawing. Folded in thirds, the invitation will fit in a legal-size envelope.

Animal Masks

What you need:
Construction paper
Crayons
Glue
Scissors
Hole punch
Reinforcements for punched holes
Pipe cleaners, 2 for each mask

Before the children arrive, cut some large circles and squares about the size of a child's face from the construction paper and leave some of the paper as rectangles. Ask the children to think of an animal whose face is made of geometric shapes. After they have chosen a basic shape for the face, have them cut medium-size geometric shapes for features like eyes, nose, and ears and tiny geometric shapes for details like pupils, inner ears, nostrils, and teeth. They can then glue the features and details onto the basic shape and add highlights in crayon.

Punch a hole on each side of the mask and glue a reinforcement on each hole. Twist the end of a pipe cleaner through each hole. Have the child put on the mask, then twist the pipe cleaners together behind their head and mark where the eyeholes should be. Have the child take off the mask and cut out the eyeholes for them.

Games

The Lion Has Escaped One child is the Lion and one the Zookeeper. The other children are in groups of 3: 2 join hands to form a cage around the third. The Lion wanders around the zoo, chased by the Zookeeper. When the Lion enters a cage to escape, the child inside must leave and become the Lion. If the Lion is caught, he and the Zookeeper change roles.

Elephant Relay Race Divide the children into 2 teams. Each child has an elephant's trunk, which is a drinking straw held in his mouth, with a round mint candy slipped on the straw. Each child in turn must run to the finish line and back without dropping the candy. If the candy falls off, the child must go back to the front of the line, get another candy, and start over. The first team to finish wins.

The Happy Lion Cake

What you need:
1 cake mix
1 can vanilla frosting
3 ounces coconut
Food coloring
1 tube chocolate decorating gel
3 licorice shoelaces
8 miniature chocolate chips
One 9-inch round cake pan
One 8-inch square cake pan
Cupcake pan
Toothpicks

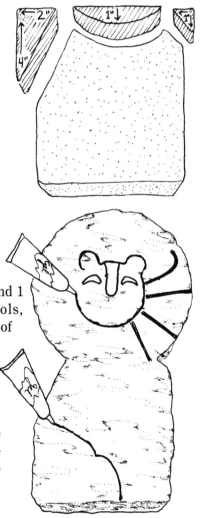

Mix the cake following package directions and bake it in one 9-inch round pan, one 8-inch square pan, and 1 cupcake pan. While the cake cools, tint half the coconut orange and half of it brown, let it dry slightly, and then toss the two lightly together. Tint the frosting a pale yellow-orange.

Level both cake layers and cut away the excess cake on the square following the diagram. Arrange the square cake below the round cake and frost the entire shape. Frost the cupcake and dip it into the coconut. Set it aside.

For the face, on the round cake with a toothpick draw a circle 2½ inches in from the outer edge. At the top, rather than completing the circle make 2 curves for the ears. For the nose, draw a rectangle starting between the ears and ending about three-quarters of the way down the face. Go over these lines with decorating gel and then draw the eyes. For the nostrils and mouth, cut six ⅜-inch pieces of licorice shoelace and arrange them as shown. Cut twelve 2- to 3-inch lengths of licorice and arrange them around the face to form the mane. Apply coconut generously to the mane, brushing it away slightly from the licorice pieces. Make the coconut as thick as you can.

On the body, draw the haunches and front paws with a toothpick, then go over the lines with decorating gel. For the tail, cut an 8-inch length of licorice. Insert 1 end into the bottom left of the square cake and the other end into the cupcake. Put 1 miniature chocolate chip on each eye and 3 on each front paw.

Tips

✔When baking a cake in different size pans, put the pans that will bake the longest in the back of the oven and the pan that will come out first in the front. Cupcakes will always be in the oven for the shortest amount of time, so place the cupcake pan in the front of the oven where you can take it out without disturbing the other cake pans.

✔To color coconut, spread it out on a piece of wax paper. In a small bowl, mix several drops of food coloring with 1 teaspoon water. Pour this on the coconut and mix it with a fork. Allow the coconut to dry.

✔Mixing Colors: To tint the frosting pale yellow-orange, use 2 generous drops of yellow food coloring and 1 scant drop of red. To tint the coconut orange, use 3 drops each of red and yellow. To tint the coconut brown, use 4 drops of yellow, 2 drops of red, and 1 of green.

A FAIRY-TALE PARTY

*F*airy tales are very old, so old in fact that nobody really knows who told the first ones. But children have listened to and been enthralled by fairy tales for as long as there have been children. And young children will be enthralled by a party with a fairy-tale theme. You can begin the festivities by sending an invitation in the form of a puzzle that the children have to solve.

At the party the children can play some traditional games and some new games and each one will have a name based on a fairy tale. For the party's finale bring out Hansel and Gretel's Cottage Cake.

For favors, buy small white boxes from your local bakery and give each child a box of enchanted objects such as seashells, pipe cleaners, colorful sponges, and perhaps a small book of your child's favorite fairy tale.

The Invitation

What you need:
Construction paper
Felt-tipped markers
Scissors

Write the party information on a piece of construction paper and draw some decorations on it. Cut the paper into jigsaw puzzle pieces and put them in an envelope to mail. The guests will have to put all the puzzle pieces together in order to read the invitation.

Games

Follow the Pied Piper This game is a variation of Follow the Leader. One child is chosen to be the Pied Piper. He or she circles the room, posturing in some way—jumping, hopping, swinging his arms, bobbing up and down. Each child must follow the Pied Piper, who then goes to the end of the line and the next child is the Pied Piper.

Who Has Cinderella's Slipper? The children sit in a circle close together. The child who is It hides her eyes while a shoe is passed around. When a parent signals, the child holding the shoe hides it—under his leg, behind his back. The child who is It guesses who has Cinderella's slipper. If she is right, she joins the circle and the child who hid the shoe becomes It.

Simple Simon Says This is the traditional game of Simon Says. One child, designated as Simple Simon, tells the children to put their hand on their head, turn around, bend over, and so forth. Only if he precedes the command with "Simple Simon Says" do the children have to do it. Otherwise they remain in the position they were in. Any child who moves at the wrong time is out. The children can take turns being Simple Simon.

Red Riding Hood and the Wolf This is a game to be played outdoors or in a large playroom. Designate one area as home base. One child is the Wolf; the other children are Red Riding Hood, the Mother, the Grandmother, the Father. Each child asks, "What time is it, Mr. Wolf?" and he replies, "One o'clock," "Three o'clock," or "Dinnertime." If he says "Dinnertime," all the children run toward home base as the Wolf chases them, saying "I'm coming to eat you." Whoever is caught before getting to home base is the next Wolf.

Is Rumpelstiltskin Your Name? All the children stand in a line opposite the child who is It. It calls out a letter that is in the name "Rumpelstiltskin" and everyone who has that letter in his or her name takes a giant step forward. It continues calling letters. The first person to reach It becomes the next It.

Clue On a tray place items that represent a favorite fairy tale. Use items such as a doll-size woman's shoe, jelly beans, an apple, bread crumbs, a man's shoe, and a small basket. See if the children can guess which fairy tale they represent: Cinderella, Jack and the Beanstalk, Snow White, Hansel and Gretel, The Elves and the Shoemaker, and Red Riding Hood. Play this game as a group so the children can help each other with the clues.

Sleeping Beauty This is a simple game to play to help quiet down the children. Have all of the children lie down on the floor, close their eyes, and pretend to be Sleeping Beauty. A parent or helper walks around and taps each child lightly on the forehead with a feather. When they are tapped they may go to the table for refreshments.

Hansel and Gretel's Cottage Cake

What you need:

2 pound cakes
1 can frosting
3 to 4 ounces coconut
Food coloring (optional)
1 tube white decorating icing
1 tube decorating gel
2 small candy canes
Chiclets or gum squares, mint leaves, gumdrops, and red hots
Miniature nonpareils and silver dragées

Level the tops of both pound cakes. Center 1 pound cake on the serving plate and frost it completely. Cut the second pound cake following the diagram. To form the roof, arrange 3 triangles upright on top of the first cake. Apply tinted or toasted coconut to the roof. Break the hooks off the candy canes and place the straight pieces upright to make the door.

Tips

✔When applying frosting, you can use not only a spatula but a butter knife, a teaspoon, a toothpick, or any kitchen utensil that helps you get the frosting onto the cake.

✔To toast coconut, line a cookie sheet with aluminum foil and place a thin layer of coconut on it. Put the cookie sheet in a preheated 325° F. oven for 8 to 10 minutes. Watch it closely so the coconut does not burn.

✔To tint coconut with food coloring, see page 40.

Outline the windows with decorating gel. Make a path from the front door with decorating icing. Place Chiclets for the front path, mint leaves and gumdrops in the frosting for trees and bushes, and red hots to outline the house. Decorate with nonpareils and silver dragées.

A PUPPET SHOW

*a*t a Puppet Show party the children can stage their own show with puppets they have made from brown paper lunch bags. Invite the children by sending them a ticket to a puppet show performed by them. A few days before the party you can make a puppet stage from a large cardboard carton. Turn the carton over and cut out the entire back and the front where the stage would be, leaving only the curtain area. Paint the curtain and top and sides of the carton with poster paint. To use the stage, place the carton on a small table and have the children stand behind it, putting their puppets on stage from the back.

When the children are making the puppets you might suggest a character from a favorite book or television show to a child who is stumped; otherwise let the children make their own creations. As they are working on the puppets they can think about what their puppet will do in the play. Depending on how many guests you have, groups of 2 or 3 children can put on a short show while the other children take turns being the audience, or all the children can put on the show for the adults.

After a round of applause for the puppeteers' great effort, reward them all with the Stage Cake and fruit punch.

The Invitation

What you need:
Construction paper
Black felt-tipped marker
Scissors

Cut a 6 x 3½-inch piece of colored construction paper. In the center of each short side cut out a 1¼-inch half-circle. On either side of the cutout circles draw a dashed line with the marker. Write "Come to a PUPPET SHOW with special performances by you for David's birthday" and below it give the party information.

The Puppets

What you need:
Brown paper
   lunch bags
Scraps of construction paper
Crepe paper streamers cut into strips
Feathers, sequins, and buttons
Felt-tipped markers
Glue or glue stick
Stapler

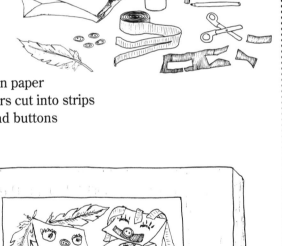

Give the children a lunch bag and show them how, by putting their hand inside the bag, the bottom of the bag becomes a face and the fold becomes the mouth. Place all of the art materials on the table and then let the children's imagination take over. When they have finished their creations, help define the puppet's body and make a tunnel for their arm by stapling the sides of the bag closed.

The Stage Cake

What you need:
1 cake mix
1 can vanilla frosting
Food coloring
2 tubes decorating gel in different colors
Cake decorations (optional)
Small animal-shaped candy
One 9 x 13-inch cake pan

Tips

✔Whenever you frost a cake using 2 or more colors, save 1 tablespoon of the original color before adding food coloring. This frosting can be used to make repairs in the design or to cover any mistakes.

✔Smooth the frosting by going over it with a spatula that has been dipped in warm water.

Bake the cake following package directions. When it is cool, lightly frost the entire shape. Set aside 1 tablespoon of frosting and add food coloring to the remainder. For the stage curtains, frost about 2 inches along the top and 3 inches along the sides. Make the curtains look as if they are pulled back. With decorating gel, write "presenting" in lowercase letters. With a contrasting color gel, write "DAVID'S BIRTHDAY" in capital letters. For the stage floor, draw lines with decorating gel. Arrange animal-shaped candy on the stage floor and sprinkle cake decorations on the curtains.

SCHOOL IS IN

*W*e all know a youngster who is looking forward to his very first day of school and his first ride on a big yellow school bus. To be in the company of all the big kids in the neighborhood means a great deal to a young child. You can capitalize on a child's anticipation by having a party to celebrate the wonderful newness of kindergarten.

To begin, send invitations in the form of an individual blackboard with each guest's name on the front. Then plan the party around a typical school day. As your opening activity have Music Time where you sing such favorites as "The Wheels on the Bus" and "The ABC Song." Next have Arts and Crafts where the children make a Happy-Sad Mask, followed by Cleanup Time where the children clean up their craft materials while singing "It's cleanup time, It's cleanup time, Time to put your things away." During Game Time play Ring Around the Rosy, Farmer in the Dell, and any of your child's favorite games. Story Time is a quiet period before you serve the food when you can read your child's favorite storybook to the guests.

Snack Time is for eating the wonderful Big Yellow School Bus Cake, served with milk in small cartons. If you prefer to have Lunch Time, you can serve the meal lunchroom style: put a wrapped sandwich and a milk carton or juice box on a small tray and give one to each child.

For party favors, give out school supplies such as a pencil box with pencils and a large eraser and a small composition book. Or you could give each child an individual-size blackboard and chalk. Put the favors in a brown paper lunch bag that has been decorated with the guest's name and gold stars.

The Invitation

What you need:
Yellow construction paper, 8 x 8½ inches
Black construction paper, 3 x 7½ inches
Chalk
Felt-tipped marker
Glue stick
Scissors

Fold the yellow construction paper in half and glue the black construction paper to the center front of it. Trim off the corners of the yellow paper diagonally ½-inch from the corner. With chalk, write "Welcome to School, Jarrod" on the black paper. Write the party information on the inside with marker.

Happy-Sad Mask

What you need:
2 white dessert-size paper plates for each child
1 empty toilet paper tube for each child
Felt-tipped markers, colored pencils, or crayons
Glue

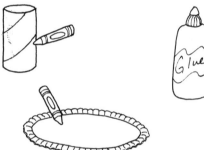

Have the children draw a happy face on one paper plate and a sad face on the other. Glue one paper plate to one side of the toilet paper tube and the other paper plate to the other side of the tube. The children can hold the toilet paper tube handle and turn the mask to show whichever emotion they choose.

Big Yellow School Bus Cake

What you need:

2 pound cakes
1 can vanilla frosting
Yellow and red food coloring
1 tube each chocolate, red, and
    blue decorating gel
1 tube white decorating icing
4 chocolate sandwich cookies
2 white Lifesavers
9 round flat candies
Wax paper
Toothpicks
Tweezers

Level both pound cakes. Cut off the front end of one cake as shown. Color the frosting by adding 8 to 10 drops of yellow and 1 scant drop of red food coloring. Put frosting between the cakes, then frost the entire shape. With a toothpick, outline the shape of the front and side windows. Fill in the areas with white decorating icing, smoothing it with a spatula. Outline the windows with chocolate decorating gel. Put two cookies on each side for wheels, then add the lines for the bumper with decorating gel. Put the Lifesavers in front for headlights.

To make the faces, place the flat round candies on a piece of wax paper and draw eyes and mouth with decorating gel. Using tweezers, place the candy faces in the windows. When the faces are on the cake, add hair with decorating gel.

Tip

✔ Cutting a cake creates many crumbs, so do not cut on the same plate or tray you plan to serve on. Put a large piece of wax paper on your table and cut the cake on it. Carefully move the cut pieces to the serving tray.

A PICNIC PARTY

a simple way to celebrate a birthday and enjoy the outdoors at the same time is to have a Picnic Party. You can have it in your own backyard or at a local park. Invite the guests by sending out an invitation that looks like a slice of watermelon with one bite missing.

Pack sandwiches and fruit in a picnic basket and bring a large thermos of lemonade. Bring a red-and-white checked tablecloth to cover a picnic table or to spread on the ground. Make cupcakes that spell out the birthday message and carry them to the picnic in a dress box lined with wax paper.

Plan some traditional games like Red Rover Red Rover, Duck Duck Goose, Red Light Green Light, and The Farmer in the Dell, but allow time for the children to play by themselves, especially if you have a child's swing, slide, or climbing equipment in your yard. If you have the party in a park, it is a good idea to ask several parents to go along to help you keep an eye on the children. Invite enough adults so you have 1 parent for every 2 or 3 children.

For favors, give each child a jar of bubbles and an interesting bubble pipe.

The Invitation

What you need:
Green and pink construction paper
Glue stick
Black felt-tipped marker
Scissors
Hole punch

Make a circle of green construction paper by tracing a plate or other round object with a 6- or 7-inch diameter; cut it out and fold it in half. Make a pink half-circle with a 5-inch diameter and cut it out. Glue

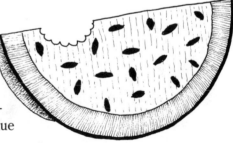

the pink half-circle on top of the folded green circle. With a black marker draw a line around the edge of the green half-circle and draw watermelon seeds in the pink area. To make the bite, place a quarter or other coin near the top left of the watermelon slice and trace around half of it. With the hole punch and making holes close together, cut out the half-circle. Write the party information on the inside.

Happy Birthday Cupcakes

What you need:
1 cake mix
1 can frosting
1 tube decorating gel
Cupcake baking pans
Paper cupcake liners

Bake the cupcakes according to package directions and when they are cool, frost them. Write the birthday message, putting 1 letter on each cupcake. On any remaining cupcakes write the age of the birthday child. Pack the cupcakes in a dress box lined with wax paper. Arrange the cupcakes in the box so they spell out the message, remember to put in candles and matches, and have the box of cupcakes be the centerpiece of your picnic table.

PARTIES
for
Children
AGES
6 TO 9

A Prehistoric Party
Chef for a Day
Design Your Own T-shirt Party
Junior Olympics
It's Magic
His Majesty's Royal Party
Play Ball!
Baseball Diamond Cake
Basketball Court Cake
You're a Star
Spring Is Here
Sail Around the World

A PREHISTORIC PARTY

*C*hildren who love dinosaurs will love a party dedicated to those prehistoric creatures. You can capture the guests' attention before the party begins by sending an invitation that looks like an archaeologist's map for discovering dinosaurs.

To decorate the party room, make a cave of brown wrapping paper. Tape the paper to the walls at the children's height and have the paper go around a corner. Make newspaper palm trees to decorate the cave. Roll up newspaper and tape the roll closed. Cut the top into strips about 1 inch wide; pull the strips down so they ressemble leaves. With poster paint, paint the leaves green and the trunks brown. Hang green crepe paper streamers above the cave.

For party favors, put a colorful plastic flashlight (for help in locating dinosaurs at night) and dinosaur stickers in a brown paper lunch bag. You can add store-bought dinosaur cookies or make your own cookies with dinosaur cookie cutters. Decorate the outside of the bags with a dinosaur sticker and the child's name. Hide the bags in a place where the children can find them during the game of Bounty Hunt.

For refreshments, serve the chocolate Dinosaur Cake and Caveperson Punch, which is milk with a little food coloring added.

The Invitation

What you need:
Typing paper
Felt-tipped markers
Small dinosaur
stickers

On a piece of typing pa-
per draw a "map" with a
trail that goes around a swamp, through a forest,
past a local landmark. At the trail's end write or type "Come to a Dinosaur Hunt at John's cave" and give the where and when of the party. Make
a photocopy of the map, one for each guest. On each copy put a small
dinosaur sticker at the trail's end near the party information. Fold the
map in thirds and then in half because children love to unfold paper.

Games

Cave Painting Put baskets or bowls of thin-line felt-tipped markers on
the floor in front of the brown-wrapping-paper cave and ask the children
to draw their own cave paintings. Begin with this game so the children
can start drawing as soon as they arrive.

Archaeologists' Dig Fill a cardboard box with plastic peanuts or other
packing material and scatter small colorful dinosaurs, at least 2 for each
child, in among the packing material. Ask the children what an archaeologist is, help them define it if necessary, then ask them to pretend they
are archaeologists and find the baby dinosaurs. Blindfold 2 children at a
time and have them search. When they have each found 2 dinosaurs, the
next children get a turn. If you have a sandbox and are having the party
outdoors, you can bury the dinosaurs in the sand. The children can add
these dinosaurs to their bags of favors at the end of the party.

The Last Dinosaur Set a kitchen timer for 2 minutes, wrap it in a towel, and hide it in the party room. Blindfold each child in turn; they have
2 minutes to find the last dinosaur alive. The other children can shout
encouragement as the finder searches by listening to the sound only.
Change the hiding place for each child.

Dinosaur Tag Four children join together to form a dinosaur by putting their hands on the waist of the person in front of them. The dinosaur tries to catch another child by making a complete circle around him. When he is caught, he joins hands and becomes the next link in the dinosaur. The game ends when everyone has been circled and is part of one long dinosaur.

Bounty Hunt The children go on a hunt looking for the hidden party bags. Play this game last, after you have served the refreshments, so when the children find the bag with their name they are ready to leave. Hide 1 or 2 bags each in several hiding places. Make a map on paper using pictures cut from magazines. For example, glue a picture of a couch, a bookshelf, a toy chest, and stereo speakers to the paper and draw a dotted line from one hiding place to the next. You will need only 4 or 5 clues if you hide a couple of the bags in each place. If the game is being played outdoors, the clues can involve the bushes and trees in the yard.

Dinosaur Cake

What you need:
1 cake mix
1 can chocolate
  frosting
About 15
  chocolate chips
4 square chocolate-covered mints
Chocolate sprinkles
1 Lifesaver
Two 8-inch round cake pans

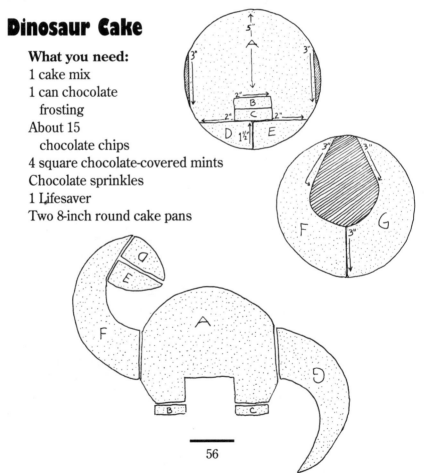

Bake the cake following package directions. When the cake is cool, level both layers. Following the diagrams at left, cut the layers and arrange the pieces to form a dinosaur. Frost the entire shape.

Cut the chocolate mint squares in quarters diagonally. Place the pieces at the edge of the cake along the neck, back, and tail. Place the chocolate chips inside the mouth for teeth and at the edge of the feet for toes. Drop the sprinkles onto the cake in selected areas to resemble scales. Place the Lifesaver for the eye and put a dot of chocolate frosting in the center for the pupil.

Tip

✔Before you cut a cake with a complex shape, insert toothpicks in the cake following the lines in the diagram. Then use another toothpick to draw the lines to be cut, making a slight indentation in the cake's surface. When you have drawn all the shapes and are satisfied with them, cut the pieces. You can always move the toothpicks if the shape is not quite right, but you cannot recut the cake.

CHEF FOR A DAY

For this party you can invite your guests to be chefs for a day and prepare their own lunch or supper; the menu is pita bread pizza, fruit punch, and birthday cake. The children will need an area such as a kitchen table where they can work. If you plan to use your dining room, in addition to covering the table you may want to protect the rug by placing a plastic tablecloth or a plastic dropcloth on the floor.

For the invitation, send the guests a menu and explain that you want them to be the chef. Before the party begins, photocopy the recipes you will be using so each child can take home a set. The children can make a toque or chef's hat before they start cooking, or you can make them before the party begins.

The children will make the cake first. Depending on the number of children you invite, you may want to make 2 recipes so there will be fewer children at each bowl. One recipe can be baked in cake pans and the other in cupcake pans. The children can eat the cake at the party and take home 2 cupcakes with their favors. While the cake and cupcakes are baking, the children can begin to assemble the pizzas and make the fruit punch. With the pizzas and punch you can serve bowls of carrot and celery sticks or a salad if you want to serve a more compete meal. After the children have eaten the pizzas, the cake and cupcakes will be cool enough to frost and decorate.

For party favors, buy colorful plastic leftover containers and write the children's names on them with a permanent felt-tipped marker. The children can take home their cupcakes in the containers as well as their hats and recipe pages.

The Invitation

What you need:
Construction paper
Felt-tipped markers
Scissors

Cut an 8 x 8½-inch piece of construction paper. Fold over 2 inches on each side so the edges of the paper meet in the center. On the front of the invitation write "Peter's Party Menu" and list the foods to be served. On the inside write "Be a Chef for a Day" and include the party information.

Peter's Party
MENU
ome to
on
Sunda
at
00 pm
Pita bread Pizza
Fruit R.S.V.P.
Punch
an d
BIRTHDAY CAKE

Chef's Toques

What you need:
White construction paper, 12 x 18 inches
White crepe paper
Felt-tipped marker
    (optional)
Glue stick
Clear tape
Stapler
Scissors

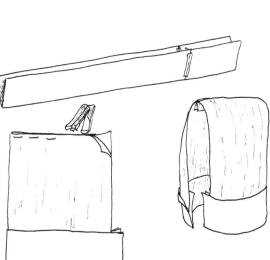

For each hat band you will need a 6 x 22-inch piece of white construction paper folded in half lengthwise to form a 3-inch cuff. To make the cuff, cut a 6 x 18-inch and a 6 x 5-inch piece of construction paper. Fold them in half lengthwise and slip one end inside the end of the other and tape them together.

Cut a 12 x 22-inch piece of crepe paper. Place 1 end inside the cuff so the edge of the crepe paper rests along the fold of the cuff, and glue it. Fold the hat in half and staple the top closed, placing the staples about 1 inch down from the top. Start stapling at the fold and stop about 1 inch from the other edge.

Fold the hat back to the original side so the stapled seam is on the inside. Bring the ends of the cuff together, slip 1 end inside the other, and tape them. You can adjust the size of the hat here by overlapping the cuff ends as much as needed. At the top seam, fold the ends of the crepe paper to the inside and tape them. Put tape along the back seam where the ends of crepe paper meet. If you like, write each child's name on the toque's cuff with a felt-tipped marker.

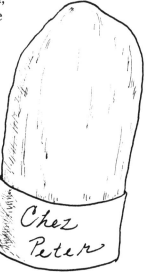

Individual Pizzas

What you need:
1 package of six 6-inch pita breads
14- or 15-ounce jar pizza sauce
12-ounce package shredded mozzarella cheese
Garlic powder and oregano to taste
Toppings: sliced pepperoni, sliced mushrooms, chopped green
     pepper, sliced zucchini, sliced tomatoes, chopped onions,
     minced garlic, bacon bits

Preheat the oven to 350° F. Have the children slice or chop the vegetables for the pizza toppings. With a sharp knife slice open the pita bread so you have 12 rounds of bread. If you like your pizza crispy, toast the bread first by putting it into the oven for a few minutes. Place the bread on aluminum foil–covered cookie sheets and put 2 tablespoons of pizza sauce on each round of bread. (If you like lots of sauce you may want to have an extra jar of pizza sauce on hand.) Have the children choose the toppings for their pizzas and put them on. Top with shredded mozzarella cheese and garlic powder and oregano to taste. Bake in the oven for 10 to 12 minutes. Provide forks and knives because the pizzas may be too heavy with toppings to pick up and eat. Makes twelve pizzas.

Fruit Punch

What you need:
6 cups grape juice
1 cup orange juice
1 tablespoon sugar
1 lemon, thinly sliced
1 orange, thinly sliced
1 apple, pared, cored, quartered, and thinly sliced
1 cup strawberries, hulled and halved
5 cups seltzer or club soda

Slice the fruit and set aside the strawberries. In a large pitcher or punch bowl mix the juices and sugar until the sugar is dissolved. Add the fruit slices. This much of the punch can be made ahead of time and refrigerated. When you are ready to serve the punch, add the club soda and strawberries. Makes about 12 cups.

The Birthday Cake

What you need:

½ cup margarine, softened
1 cup sugar
2 eggs
1 teaspoon vanilla
2 cups sifted flour
2 teaspoons baking powder
¼ teaspoon salt
¾ cup milk
Two 8-inch round cake pans
1 can frosting
Decorating gel
Cake decorations and sprinkles

> ## Tip
>
> ✔To make decorating easier, open the packages of cake decorations and sprinkles and divide each one into several custard dishes or other small bowls. Place these bowls and several tubes of decorating gel around your table so each child can have a variety of decorations within easy reach.

Preheat the oven to 350° F. Grease the cake pans. Beat the softened margarine and sugar together. Add the eggs and vanilla and beat until the mixture is fluffy. Sift together the flour, baking powder, and salt and add alternately with the milk. Pour the batter into the greased cake pans and bake for 25 minutes or until a toothpick inserted in the center comes out clean.

If you make cupcakes, bake them for 15 minutes or until a toothpick inserted in the center comes out clean.

When the cake is cool, place 1 layer on a plate and frost the top. Put the second layer on top and frost the entire cake. Let the children have fun creating a masterpiece with decorating gel, sprinkles, and decorations.

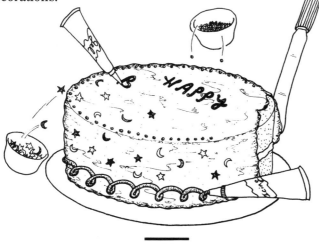

DESIGN YOUR OWN T-SHIRT PARTY

*C*hildren love to create and what better way to show off their creativity than to wear their very own designs proudly on a T-shirt. For this party you will need enough space for the children to work; you can have them spread out on the floor if you do not have enough space at the table. Give each child several newspapers to work on so the floor or table is protected from any spills. On the invitation you can let the children know that they will be designing a T-shirt and suggest that they come dressed appropriately.

For refreshments serve the T-shirt Cake with Ice-Cream Cup Place Cards and fruit punch. For party favors, in addition to their T-shirts, you can give each child an artist's kit containing some of the following items: felt-tipped markers, poster paints, stencils, drawing pencils, and a drawing pad.

The Invitation

What you need:
Construction paper,
   8 x 8½-inch rectangle
Felt-tipped markers
Scissors

Fold the rectangle in half lengthwise. Draw a paintbrush on the rectangle with a pencil. Make the bristles and the body of the paintbrush each about 3 inches long, then draw the handle. Trace over the design with a felt-tipped marker. Cut out the paintbrush handle at the bottom and trim the bristles in a zigzag at the top. Write "Elizabeth's Design Your Own T-shirt Party" on the body of the paintbrush and write the party information on the inside.

The T-shirts

What you need:
1 white cotton T-shirt for each child (boys' undershirts work well)
Tubes of fabric paint in a variety of colors and textures
Paintbrushes
Pieces of lightweight cardboard
Pencils

Place a piece of lightweight cardboard between the front and back of each T-shirt so the paint will not penetrate through to the back of the shirt.

Have some pictures to stimulate the children's imagination. Try a mixture of popular items like a dinosaur, ballet slippers, animals, and flowers, as well as abstract and geometric designs from wallpaper and wrapping paper.

Have the children draw their design in pencil first so they can adjust and change it. They can apply the fabric paint directly from the tube or use a paintbrush for a special effect. (Have a couple of extra T-shirts on hand in case a child becomes disillusioned by a design that went awry.) Set the T-shirts aside to dry as the children play games and have refreshments. If the shirts are very wet, you may suggest that they leave them overnight and you will deliver them the next day.

Ice-Cream Cup Place Cards

What you need:
Ice cream
Butter cookies
1 tube decorating icing or gel
Sprinkles (optional)
Cupcake pans
Paper cupcake liners

A day or two before the party, line cupcake pans with paper liners and place a scoop of ice cream in each one. Top with sprinkles if you like and freeze until firm. Remove the paper cups from the cupcake tins, place them in a plastic bag, and return to the freezer. For the place cards, with decorating icing write each child's name on a sturdy butter cookie or biscuit. Take the ice-cream cups out of the freezer about 10 to 15 minutes before you plan to serve them and gently push a cookie into the top of each softened scoop.

For variety you can put chocolate cookie crumbs in the bottom of the cupcake liners before you put in the scoop of ice cream. Or drizzle a small amount of chocolate syrup on top of the ice cream and add chopped nuts or toasted coconut to make a small sundae.

T-shirt Cake

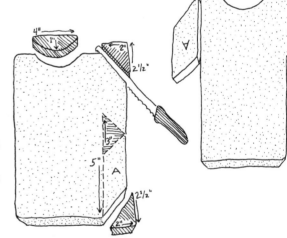

What you need:
1 cake mix
1 can frosting
1 or more tubes
  decorating gel
Small multicolored
  candy or large
  cake decorations
One 9 x 13-inch
  cake pan
Toothpicks

Bake the cake following package directions. When it is cool, mark with toothpicks the points shown on the diagram and cut out the pieces. Put the second sleeve in place and frost the shape. With decorating gel out-

64

line the T-shirt shape and write "Happy Birthday Elizabeth." Decorate the T-shirt with the decorating gel and cake decorations or small candy.

JUNIOR OLYMPICS

This is a party for active children and one that is best held outdoors. The children can run, jump, throw a Frisbee, and toss a ball all afternoon. Although the nature of the Olympics is competition, you may want to explain to the children that the games are all in good fun and that prizes will be awarded at a special ceremony at the end of the party. And then plan lots of team games so the focus is not on individual winners.

Ask 2 parents or 2 teenage friends to serve as referees. They can wear shorts and matching striped shirts, if you like, and carry whistles around their necks to blow at the start of each game. They can help set up and take down the games and generally keep things moving. Have lots of juice or punch on hand during the games for thirsty players.

When the games are over, make a formal presentation of the awards. Play the score to the movie *Chariots of Fire* as the children march around the backyard and then seat themselves in front of the stage, a cardboard carton turned upside down. Take an instant photograph of each child as the medal is placed around his or her neck. At the conclusion of the ceremony, serve the Podium Cake and ice cream to all the winners. For favors, give each child a whistle, a pink rubber ball, a sun visor or sweatband, a bag of foil-covered chocolate coins, and, of course, their medal and photograph.

A day or two before the party, gather the props for the games, choose the winning categories, and make the medals. For each medal you will need a 2-foot length of ribbon and a foil-covered chocolate coin. Make a loop with the ribbon and glue the ends to the back of the coin. Have 1 for each child. Think of categories for winners that emphasize the good fun of the games rather than individual talent. Award the medals to the most sporting, the funniest, the child who stayed the cleanest, the child who got the dirtiest, the child who laughed the most, the child who listened most intently, the child who challenged the rules most often.

The Invitation

What you need:
White and
   dark-colored
   construction paper
Orange cellophane
   paper
Felt-tipped marker
Clear tape
Glue stick
Scissors

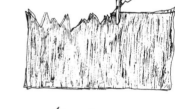

For the handle, cut a 5 x 6-inch rectangle from white and a dark color construction paper. Fold each in half and slip the white paper inside the dark paper so that when you cut the torch shape both pieces of paper will be exactly the same shape. Draw a torch and cut it out. Take out the white paper and set it aside.

Cut 2 pieces of cellophane, each 6 x 12 inches. Cut uneven points into one long side of each piece. Gather the other uncut long side of the cellophane paper and tape it to the front of the torch on the inside. Gather the second piece of cellophane and tape it to the back of the torch on the inside of the invitation. Using glue stick, glue the white torch inside the dark torch so it covers the taped ends of cellophane. On the front of the torch with marker write "Carry the torch . . ." and on the inside write ". . . to a Junior Olympics Party" and give the party information. The invitation will fit in a legal-size envelope for mailing.

Let the Games Begin

Three-legged Race Have each child choose a partner and tie the children's inside legs together with a scarf or ace bandage. Divide them into teams and have them race to the finish line. The first team across is the winner.

Potato Race Divide the children into teams. Give the first player in each team a large serving spoon with a potato on it. The child race-walks to the finish line and back and gives the spoon and potato to the next child in line. The first team to finish wins.

Hop, Skip, and a Jump Divide the racecourse into thirds. Divide the children into teams. Have each child hop on 1 foot for the first third of the race, skip the second third, and jump with 2 feet to the finish line. First team to finish wins.

Ball Toss Divide the children into 2 teams. Set up 2 containers such as laundry baskets or cardboard cartons. Give the first children in line a tennis ball. Each child in turn runs to a line several feet in front of the basket, tosses the ball until he gets a basket, retrieves the ball, and runs back. The first team to finish wins.

Obstacle Race Between the start and finish lines set up 2 sets of obstacles: a small carton to jump over, a Hula-Hoop to spin around the waist, a tent-shaped piece of cardboard to crawl under, and an inflatable tube to put over their head and slip down their body. Children must maneuver each obstacle and run back to the start. First team to finish wins.

Tug-of-War End the games with a final game of tug-of-war. Use a length of clothesline and divide the children into teams. Mark the center on the grass with chalk. The first team to pull the other over the center line wins.

The Podium Cake

What you need:
1 cake mix
1 can frosting
3 small rectangular biscuit
  cookies
Decorating icing and gel
  in several colors
One 9-inch and one 8-inch
  round cake pan
One 6- or 7-ounce tuna fish can
3 craft sticks
Aluminum foil

Wash out the tuna fish can thoroughly so it does not smell of fish. Line it with aluminum foil and grease the foil when you grease the cake pans. Make the cake following the package directions, baking it in the 2 round pans and the tuna fish can. Bake the tuna fish can for about 20 minutes (test it with a toothpick) and the 2 round pans for the amount of time indicated on the package directions. Allow the cakes to cool.

To make the flags, decorate the cookies with decorating icing and decorating gel. Attach them to the craft sticks by putting a small amount of decorating icing on one end of the craft stick and gently pressing the decorated cookie onto the craft stick. Set the flags aside and allow the decorating icing to harden slightly.

Level all 3 cake layers. Place the 9-inch layer on the plate and frost the top. Place the 8-inch layer on top of it and frost it. Place the smallest layer on top and frost the entire shape. Insert the flags by gently pushing the craft sticks into the top of the cake.

Tip

✔When making the flag cookies, remember that decorating icing is thicker and holds its shape whereas decorating gel is more fluid and fills an area more easily. To make the American flag, draw lines with red and white decorating icing except in the upper left corner. Fill that area with blue decorating gel. For the stars, use a pair of tweezers to place white sprinkles in rows. For some of the flags you can use food coloring to paint a design on white icing or use small candies for the details. The center of the Japanese flag can be a red M&M.

IT'S MAGIC

*M*agic is illusion. Magic is having fast hands and a faster mind. But most of all, magic is fun. A performance of magic tricks is great entertainment for a room full of partygoers. You can ask a friend to perform at the party or hire a high school or college student who is an amateur magician to put on a short show. You'll want to leave time for the children to learn some tricks of their own that you or the magician can teach them. Below are a few magic tricks to get you started. Be sure to practice them beforehand.

After the children have mastered some of the tricks you can serve refreshments, the Out-of-the-Hat Cake and ice cream and soda.

For party bags, give out brown paper lunch bags on which you have drawn a magician's hat and written each child's name: "Alexandra's Bag of Tricks." In the bag have the supplies needed to perform the tricks shown here: a deck of cards, a piece of construction paper, 2 paper clips, and a dollar bill, as well as small tricks such as the disappearing penny that you can purchase at a party store or variety store.

The Invitation

What you need:
A deck of cards
Construction paper
Glue
Felt-tipped marker
Pencil
Scissors

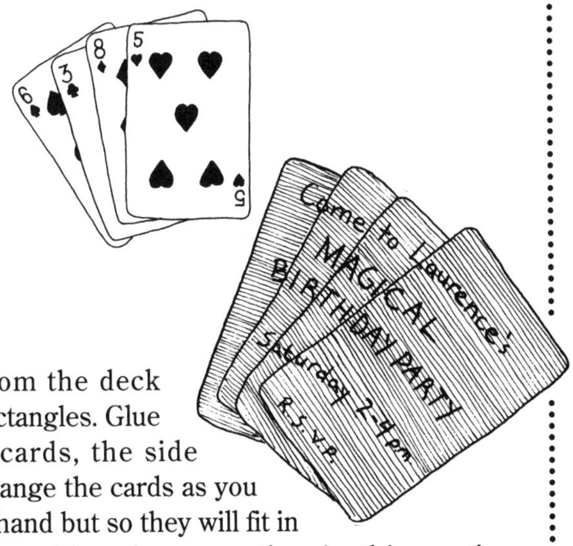

Trace around 1 card from the deck 4 times and cut out the rectangles. Glue them to the back of 4 cards, the side without the numbers. Arrange the cards as you would hold them in your hand but so they will fit in a standard-size envelope. Glue them together in this postion. With a marker write the party information on the construction paper side.

The Magic Tricks

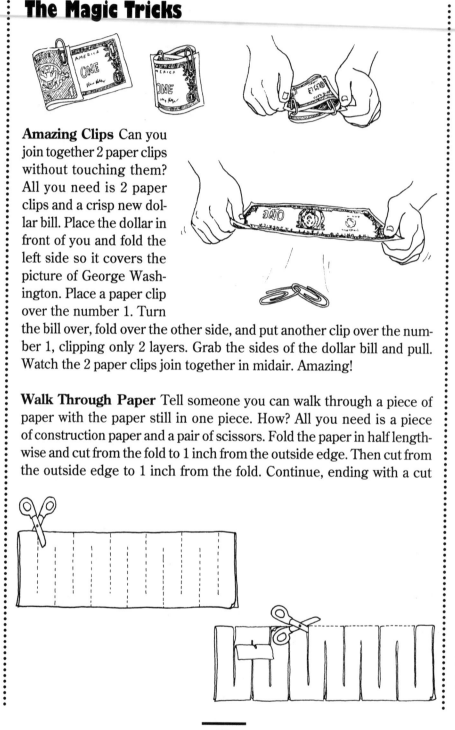

Amazing Clips Can you join together 2 paper clips without touching them? All you need is 2 paper clips and a crisp new dollar bill. Place the dollar in front of you and fold the left side so it covers the picture of George Washington. Place a paper clip over the number 1. Turn the bill over, fold over the other side, and put another clip over the number 1, clipping only 2 layers. Grab the sides of the dollar bill and pull. Watch the 2 paper clips join together in midair. Amazing!

Walk Through Paper Tell someone you can walk through a piece of paper with the paper still in one piece. How? All you need is a piece of construction paper and a pair of scissors. Fold the paper in half lengthwise and cut from the fold to 1 inch from the outside edge. Then cut from the outside edge to 1 inch from the fold. Continue, ending with a cut from the folded edge just like the first cut. Cut the folds at the folded edge except for the first and last ones. Open the paper and you can walk through it.

Whose Birthday Is It? Have a bowl and slips of paper in front of you. Ask the children whose birthday was last month and whose is next month and so on. As they call out their names, pretend to write them each on a slip of paper but actually write the birthday child's name. Fold each slip of paper as soon as you have written on it and place it in the bowl. When you have 8 or 10 names in the bowl, tell the children that you know whose birthday it is today. Ask 1 child to reach in to choose a slip of paper and read the answer aloud. She will read the birthday child's name no matter which slip of papers she chooses.

Pick a Card Ask a friend to pick a card. He should look at it but not show it to you. While he studies the card, gather the cards together, bring them behind your back, and turn the bottom card over. Turn the deck over quickly and bring it to the front again. It will look like the entire deck is face down but only the top card actually is. Have your friend put the card face down back into the deck. Put the deck behind your back and turn the bottom card over again quickly as you say some magical words like "Abracadabra." Bring the cards to the front, spread them out, and watch the surprise as the card that was chosen appears face up.

71

Out-of-the-Hat Cake

What you need:

1 cake mix
1 can dark chocolate frosting
¼ cup fruit-flavored jam
Three 8-inch round cake pans
Lightweight cardboard, 9-inch square
Wax paper
White and pink construction paper
Toothpicks
Glue stick
Glue
Scissors

Make the cake following package directions and bake it in three 8-inch layers. Reduce the baking time given on the package by 5 minutes.

While the cakes cool, cut a 9-inch circle from the cardboard using a compass or tracing around a plate. Cut a 6½-inch circle from the center so you have a 1¼-inch-wide ring. This will be the hat brim. Cut the same size ring from wax paper and attach it to the cardboard with the glue stick. Cut white ears and pink inner ears from construction paper. Put glue down the center of the white ears. Place a toothpick on the ear so the bottom half extends below the ear. Glue the pink inner ear on top of the white ear, sandwiching the toothpick between.

Assemble the 3 cake layers, putting jam between them. Frost the cake with chocolate frosting. Cover the ring with chocolate frosting and place it on the cake. Smooth the frosting on the cake and the ring so they look like one piece. Place the rabbit ears in the center of the cake.

Tip

✔If you want the birthday greetings to look as if they are coming out of the top of the hat, write the message on a piece of paper, glue it to a toothpick, and insert the toothpick into the top of the cake.

HIS MAJESTY'S ROYAL PARTY

a party where the guests can dress up as noble knights and love-ly ladies is a great choice for children who love the King Arthur tales. You can set the mood for the party by sending invitations in the form of a royal proclamation from the King (if the birthday child is a boy) or Queen (from a girl). Decorate the room with a brown-wrapping-paper castle that the children can decorate themselves. At the party the children can make a crown or hat; the boys can also make a shield, the girls a scepter.

For party favors make a Treasure Box for each child by covering a toddler-size shoe box with gold foil wrapping paper. Wrap the top and bottom separately so the box can be opened without being unwrapped. The favors can be small toys and candy all wrapped in aluminum foil. Hide the treasure boxes before the party begins and the children can find them during the last game. The spectacular Castle Cake makes a fitting end for such a royal party.

The Invitation

What you need:
Construction paper, 1 piece for each child
Foil gift-wrapping paper
⅓ yard ribbon, ½-inch wide
Felt-tipped markers
Scissors
Glue stick

Make a border by drawing a line with a pencil 1 inch in from the edges of the construction paper. Round the corners by tracing around a small glass. Draw over the border with a marker. Cut a 2-inch circle from the foil wrapping paper and cut a 4-inch length of ribbon. Fold the ribbon in half to make a V. Put the point of the ribbon V under the circle and glue the circle to the bottom right corner of the paper. Write "Royal Proclamation" at the top and "The Queen (or King) invites you to her palace for a party" and add the party information. Roll up the paper and tie it with the remaining ribbon. You can hand-deliver the invitation or roll it up tightly and mail it in a legal-size envelope.

Royal Crown

What you need:
Gold- or silver-colored poster cardboard
Felt-tipped markers
Chiclets
Aluminum foil
Coin
Glue stick
Clear tape
Scissors

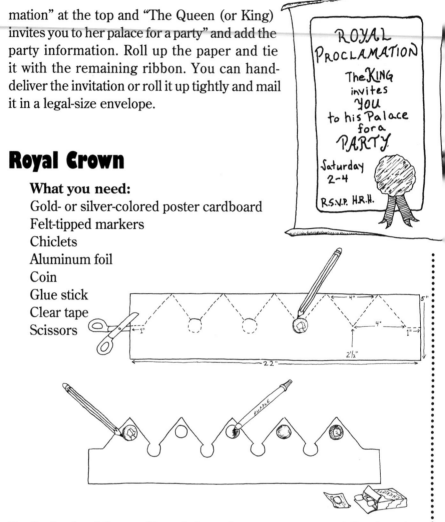

On the back of the cardboard draw the crown pattern, following the diagram. Place a coin—a quarter is a good size—on the bottom points of the crown, trace around, and then cut around the circle. On the front side of the crown place the quarter below each point and trace around it. With marker color in these circles and draw a line above the base of the crown. Cover the Chiclets with aluminum foil and glue them onto the circles. Fit the crown onto the child's head and secure the ends with tape.

Hat for a Prince or Princess

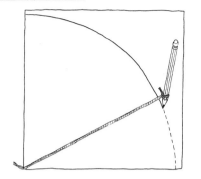

What you need:
Colorful poster cardboard
Gold or silver foil
  gift-wrapping paper
Gold star stickers
Gold or silver curling ribbon
Hole punch (optional)
Elastic thread
Clear tape
Glue stick
Pencil-and-string compass
Scissors

With a piece of string tied to a pencil, draw a quarter-circle with a 16-inch radius on poster cardboard. Cut it out. Cut out large stars from foil wrapping paper. Glue the large stars and attach star stickers on the quarter-circle. Cut three 30-inch lengths of ribbon, curl them, and attach them to the inside of the point with clear tape. Roll the quarter-circle into a cone and secure the seam with clear tape. (It is easier to roll a cone shape if you first fold the point in half vertically.) Punch a hole in either side of the cone with a hole punch or the point of the scissors, thread a 10-inch length of elastic thread through the holes, and knot the thread ends.

Shield

What you need:
Gold- or silver-colored poster cardboard
Felt-tipped markers
Clear tape
Scissors

Cut out the shield shape and handle from cardboard, following the diagram. Have the children decorate the shield with markers. Fold the han-

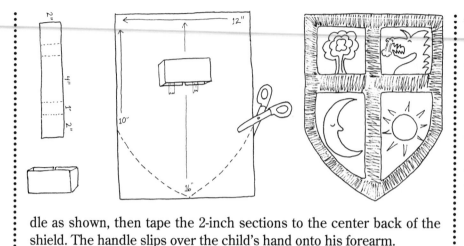

dle as shown, then tape the 2-inch sections to the center back of the shield. The handle slips over the child's hand onto his forearm.

Scepter

What you need:
Poster cardboard
Drinking straws
Aluminum foil
Silver curling ribbon
Glue stick
Clear tape
Scissors

Cut out 4-inch stars from the cardboard and cover them with aluminum foil. Cut a 24-inch length of ribbon, fold it in half, and curl the ends. Tape the folded end of the ribbon and the end of a straw to the back of one star. Glue the other star on top of it.

Games

Decorate the Castle The children can decorate the castle as they arrive. Cut 3 pieces of brown wrapping paper, one 5 x 2½ feet for the castle and two 1-foot-square pieces for the turrets. Put the turrets at the top corners, draw a door with a rounded top in the center bottom, and hang the castle on the wall. Cut pennants from colored construction paper, glue to a straw, and let them fly from the top of the castle's turrets. Have bowls of markers for the children to use to decorate the castle.

Good Morning Your Majesty The King or Queen sits in a chair blindfolded. Each child says "Good Morning Your Majesty," disguising his or her voice. If the King or Queen cannot guess who it is, that child gets to be the next King or Queen.

Message Puzzle Write a message such as "A castle good enough to eat awaits you in the dining room" on lightweight cardboard and cut it into pieces like a puzzle. Hide the pieces around the room but in plain sight and have the guests find and complete the puzzle.

Treasure Hunt Hide the Treasure Boxes of party favors in a place where the children won't see them, such as in your hall coat closet or in the bathtub with the shower curtain closed. Write clues to finding them on separate pieces of paper. Give the guests the first clue: "You may find a goody pouch under the couch." Under the couch they will find the second clue: "Look for treasure behind the instrument of musical pleasure." Behind the piano they will find the third clue. The fourth or fifth clue should lead them to the boxes. Have the children play this game last after the cake has been served so they are ready to leave as soon as they have found the Treasure Boxes.

Castle Cake

What you need:
2 cake mixes
1 can chocolate frosting
½ cup fruit-flavored jam
4 empty ice-cream cones
Chocolate sugar wafer cookies
Miniature nonpareil candies
Two 4-inch pieces of licorice shoelace
Two 9 x 13-inch cake pans
4 empty toilet paper tubes
Brown construction paper or brown wrapping paper
3 x 4-inch piece of red construction paper
2½ x 6-inch piece of cardboard
Glue
Toothpicks
Scissors

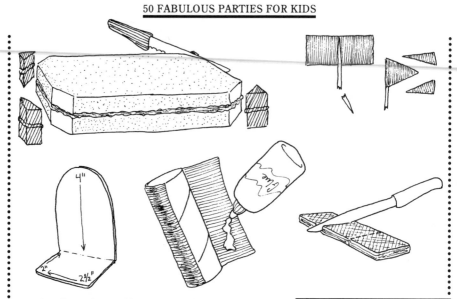

Bake the cakes following package directions. If you do not have 2 cake pans, bake 1 cake and when it is cool bake the second cake. While the cakes are baking, make the turrets. Cut four 4½ x 6-inch pieces of brown paper. Wrap each one around a toilet paper tube and glue in place. Allow the glue to dry.

When the cakes are cool, level the tops. Spread jam on top of 1 cake and place the second cake on top of it. Cut off 1 inch diagonally from each corner, then frost the entire shape.

For the castle entrance, round 1 end of the piece of cardboard by placing a drinking glass on the cardboard and tracing around it. Cut out the rounded shape. Fold the cardboard 4 inches down from the top so you have a door and a drawbridge. Cover 1 side of the door and drawbridge with chocolate frosting and place it in the center of 1 long side of the cake. Outline the door with nonpareils. Insert 1 end of each of the licorice shoelaces into the cake on either side of the door; put the bottom ends next to the drawbridge.

For the turrets, place the covered toilet

Tips

✔The Castle Cake is quite heavy. For a serving tray use a sturdy wooden tray or a double thickness of cardboard covered with aluminum foil.

✔While the cake is baking, make all of the decorations for the cake: the turrets, cut out the cardboard for the door and drawbridge, the pennants, cut the sugar wafer cookies into thirds using a sharp knife. You will need about 7 cookies, but have extra on hand in case some of them crumble.

✔When you move the Castle Cake, carry it without the turrets and put them in place once the cake is on the table. If the turrets should fall over, the ice-cream cones will break.

paper tubes at each of the cutout corners of the cake. Put a small amount of frosting along the rim of each of the ice-cream cones and put the cones upside down on top of the tubes. To make the pennants, cut four 1 x 3-inch pieces of construction paper, fold them in half, cut a point at one end, and open them up. Cut or break off the bottom one-third of 4 tooth-picks. Place a shortened toothpick on the fold line, add glue, and fold in half. Put a small amount of frosting on the end of each toothpick and place them on the points of the ice-cream cones.

For the crenellations, cut the chocolate sugar wafers into thirds and place them around the top edge of the cake. Place miniature nonpareils in the frosting below the cookies.

PLAY BALL!

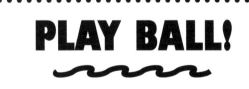

*J*f your child is an avid sports fan and particpates in organized games, you can give a party for the team after the last game as a way to congratulate the young players for a well-played season. Invite the team back to your house and serve a cake that depicts their playing field.

Decorate the party room with crepe paper streamers in the team's colors and make a sign saying "Congratulations team." If you or one of the other parents have taken videos of the team, play highlights for the children. As party favors, give a soccer player's survival kit: a miniature duffle bag with a can of Gatorade, a candy bar, and a sweatband inside.

This party can easily be adapted for a child's birthday. Invite friends to come play soccer at your house (if your yard is large enough) or at a local park. Bring everyone back to your house for refreshments. Make sure to mention in the sneaker-shaped invitations that the children should wear clothing that is appropriate for playing the sport.

The Invitation

What you need:
Construction paper
¼-inch wide ribbon
Glue stick
Black felt-tipped marker
Scissors
Hole punch

Cut an 11 x 3½-inch piece of construction paper and fold it in half. With the fold on top, round off the bottom edge. Punch 2 rows of 4 holes, making the first row 1¼ inches from the bottom edge and the rest of the holes ¾-inches apart. Cut a 24-inch length of ribbon, lace it through the holes, and tie it in a bow. On the inside, secure the ribbon in two or three places with the glue stick. With marker draw a line around the edge of the sneaker top and draw a toe cap. Write "Lace Up Your Sneakers and Play Ball!" on the inside along with the party information.

Soccer Field Cake

What you need:
1 cake mix
1 can vanilla frosting
Green food coloring
1 tube chocolate decorating gel
One 9 x 13-inch cake pan
Construction paper: red, white, and brown
Toothpicks
Glue stick
Dental floss
Scissors

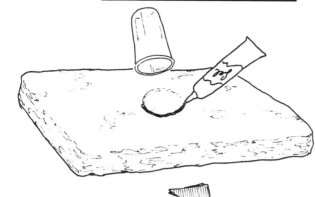

Bake the cake following package directions and let it cool. Add 2 or 3 drops of green food coloring to the frosting to make it light grass green. Frost the cake. Draw the playing field on the cake, following the diagrams, and go over the lines with chocolate decorating gel (see Tip on page 82).

To make the flags, cut 5 white and 5 red 1 x 2-inch rectangles from construction paper. Fold the red rectangle in half; with the fold on your left, cut from the bottom right to the upper left corner. Open the red triangle and glue it on top of the white rectangle. Fold this rectangle in half, then open it up. Place a toothpick on the fold so most of the toothpick hangs below the rectangle. Apply glue and fold it again. Insert the toothpick into the cake.

To make the scoreboard, cut a 3 x 10-inch rectangle from brown paper and fold it in half. Open it up and glue a toothpick to each of the bottom corners. Fold the rectangle over and glue in place. Cut a 2¾ x 4½-inch rectangle from white paper.

To make the goalposts, cut 2 trape-

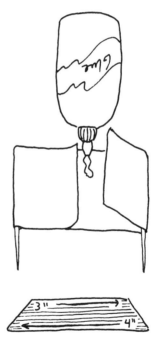

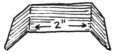

zoids (see diagram on preceding page) from brown construction paper. Fold on the fold lines and place on the cake.

Write the birthday greetings in block letters on the paper. Or if you have a computer, compose the birthday message on the computer so it resembles a computerized scoreboard. Cut out the message and glue it to the brown paper scoreboard. Place it along one long side of the cake.

> ### Tip
>
> ✔To draw a straight line on a cake, use a piece of dental floss held taut between your hands and make an impression in the frosting. To make a circle or half circle, press a drinking glass lightly into the frosting. For the playing fields shown here, use a glass that is 2 to 2½ inches in diameter. Draw over all the lines with decorating gel.

Baseball Diamond Cake

What you need:
1 cake mix
1 can vanilla frosting
1 tube chocolate
   decorating gel
5 square chocolate-covered
   candies
One 8-inch square cake pan
Cupcake pans
Dental floss

Bake the cake, making 1 square cake and 12 cupcakes. When the cake is cool, level the top of the square. Frost the cake and the cupcakes. With dental floss, make the straight lines. Place the candies in the corners for the bases and in the center for the pitcher's mound. Draw over the lines with decorating gel. On the cupcakes draw the seams of a baseball with decorating gel and place them around the cake. Make a scoreboard as described for the Soccer Field Cake and insert it into the cake or into 2 cupcakes.

Basketball Court Cake

What you need:
1 cake mix
1 can frosting
Food coloring
1 tube chocolate decorating gel
4 peppermint sticks
2 rectangular butter cookies
One 9 x 13-inch cake pan
Dental floss

Bake the cake following the package directions. While the cake is baking, make the backboards. On 1 rectangular cookie with decorating gel make 2 rectangles, 1 just inside the edge of the cookie and another, smaller 1 inside the first. Using a small amount of frosting as glue, glue the cookie to 2 peppermint sticks. Make 1 backboard for each end of the court and allow the frosting to set as the cake cools.

When the cake is cool, level it. With food coloring tint the frosting a light brownish-orange color so it looks like a wood floor and frost the entire cake. Draw the lines on the court with chocolate decorating gel and insert the backboards on either end. Make a scoreboard following the directions given on page 81.

YOU'RE A STAR

a party that celebrates the future stars of America may stimulate the children's thoughts about their future and the many possibilities open to them. Ask the children to come dressed as the celebrity they would like to be—a movie star, an athlete, the first woman president, or the scientist who finds a cure for cancer.

To decorate the room you can hang stars from the ceiling and have mock-ups of magazine covers on the walls. Cut stars from yellow construction paper, cover with glue, and sprinkle on glitter. When the glue dries, attach a piece of string and hang the stars from the ceiling.

For the magazine covers honoring the children, cut cover logos from magazines such as *Time, Newsweek, People,* and your local paper's Sunday magazine. Use candid snapshots or school photographs, make enlarged or same-size photocopies of the pictures. Glue a magazine logo to the top of a piece of construction paper, then glue a child's photograph in the center. With a marker write "*Time* Magazine's Teacher of the Year," "*Newsweek*'s Most Highly Rated TV Anchor," "*Scientific American*'s Scientist of the Decade," "*The New Yorker*'s Best New Writer," and the "*Sport's Illustrated*'s Most Talented College Athlete," and so on. Hang these magazine covers on the walls.

At the party you can take an instant photograph of each child and have them make a star-studded frame for it. After they have played the games, serve the Star Cake and individual cupcakes. The children can take home their frames, the magazine covers, and a bag of small favors.

The Invitation

What you need:
Black or dark blue construction paper
Typing paper
Star stickers
Gold foil gift-wrapping paper
Felt-tipped markers
Glue stick
Scissors

Cut an 8 x 8½-inch piece of construction paper and fold it in half. Cut out a 2½-inch star from the foil wrapping paper and glue it on the front of the invitation. Add some star stickers. Glue a 3¾ x 8-inch piece of typing paper to the inside and write "You're a Star" and the party information. Explain that you want the children to come dressed as the celebrity they would like to be, such as a Pulitzer Prize–winning novelist, a diplomat who helps bring peace between East and West, or the next Wimbledon tennis champion.

Star Picture Frames

What you need:
An instant camera and film
Lightweight cardboard or posterboard,
    cut into 4¾-inch squares
Craft sticks, 10 for each frame
Glitter and sequins
Star stickers
Glue

Take an instant photograph of each child. To make the frame, glue a craft stick to 2 opposite sides of the cardboard square making sure that there is enough room for the photograph to be slipped in between the sticks. Then glue a craft stick at the top and bottom of the square so the ends of these sticks rest on the vertical sticks. Repeat, alternating sticks along the sides and top and bottom until you have 2 or 3 sticks on each side and 2 on top and bottom. Decorate the sticks with glitter, sequins, and star stickers. Allow the glue to dry while the children play games and have the cake. Before the children leave, slip the instant photograph inside the frame from the top or bottom.

Games

Who Am I? Each child chooses a celebrity they want to be but they do not tell anyone their choice. The children ask each child in turn questions that can be answered with a yes or no such as "Are you a man?," "Do you sing?," "Do you play guitar?" The one who guesses correctly gets to be the next celebrity. If the child stumps the group, she reveals who she is and chooses the next child to be questioned.

Going to Hollywood One child begins by saying, "Went to Hollywood and picked up an apple." The second child repeats the sentence and adds an item that begins with a *b*. Each child repeats what has been said before and adds an item that begins with the next letter of the alphabet. If a child can't repeat the list, he drops out of the game.

Charades Divide the children into 2 groups. Play a traditional game of Charades using the names of movies, books, television shows, and songs.

Outrageous People You will need typing paper and pencils. Fold pieces of typing paper in thirds horizontally and give 1 to each child. Ask the children to draw a head on the top section and then fold it to the back and pass it to the child on their right. Each child should then draw a torso and arms in the middle section, fold it to the back, and pass it on. On the third section the children will draw legs and feet. Unfold the papers and pass them around so everyone can see the bizarre creations. The children can name them after the people they most resemble.

Star Cake

What you need:
1 cake mix
1 can vanilla or lemon frosting
1 tube yellow decorating gel
Colored sugar crystals
One 8-inch square cake pan and cupcake pans

Mix the cake following package directions and make one 8-inch square cake and 12 cupcakes. When the cake is cool, cut it following the diagram. Arrange the pieces to form a star, placing the triangles so the points that were on the outside of the square are now on the outside of the star,

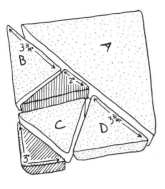

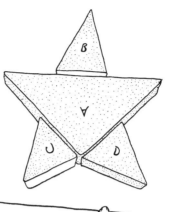

as shown. Frost the cake. Outline the shape and write your message with decorating gel. Frost the cupcakes and draw a star on top with decorating gel. Sprinkle both cake and cupcakes with yellow-colored sugar crystals.

Tip

✔ When you frost the sides of the Star Cake, start at the inner points and work out to the outer point. Gently apply frosting around the outer points.

SPRING IS HERE

The glorious flowers of spring are the first harbinger of warm weather. Planting these flowers as well as fruits and vegetables and watching them grow is very exciting for children.

To set the mood for this party, send a packet of flower seeds as the invitation. In the invitation you may want to suggest that the children wear play clothes to the party so they will feel free to dig in the dirt.

At the party, the children can plant seeds and make a planter. Have the children make the planter first so the glue can dry while they plant their seeds. Allow some time for cleanup so the children can wash the dirt off their hands before you bring out the Butterfly Cake.

For party favors, give each child a colorful plastic watering can or a trowel and another packet of seeds. The children will also take home their planters and their plants.

The Invitation

What you need:
1 packet of seeds per child
8 x 8½-inch piece of
    construction paper
Felt-tipped markers
Pencil
Scissors

Fold the construction paper in half. Trace over the seed packet, cut slits in the corners of the outline, and insert the corners of the seed packet under the slits. (If you glue the seed packet to the invitation, the person who receives it will not be able to read the instructions on the back.) With a marker write "Spring Is Here" or another message above the seed packet. Write the party information inside. Ask the children to wear play clothes to the party so they can play in the dirt.

Decoupage Planters

What you need:
Empty cans, 17-ounce size or larger, with smooth sides
Pictures of flowers from magazines, seed catalogs, or seed packets
White glue
Scissors

Choose cans that are short and stout, such as a can that nuts come in, rather than tall and thin cans. Place a small flowerpot or yogurt container inside the can to make sure the container fits. Remove any paper label from the can. Cut pictures of flowers from catalogs or magazines. To create interesting shapes, cut around the large flowers so no background shows. Apply these pictures to the sides of the can with glue, overlapping the pictures so the can is completely covered. Allow the glue to dry.

Radish Plants

What you need:
Small containers such as small flowerpots
    or empty 8-ounce yogurt containers
Fish tank gravel
Soil
Radish seeds

Radish seeds are a good choice for children because they sprout so quickly. You can plant some seeds a few days before the party so the children can see what the plants look like. Or plant enough containers so that each child can take home a sprouted plant as well as their own newly planted seeds.

Put gravel in the bottom of the container and add soil. Press the seeds down into the top of the soil and water them.

Butterfly Cake

What you need:
1 cake mix
1 can frosting
1 tube decorating icing
1 or more tubes decorating gel
Two 8-inch square cake pans
2 pipe cleaners
Toothpicks

Bake the cake following package directions. Each butterfly is made from 1 square layer. When the cake is cool, cut each square in half diagonally

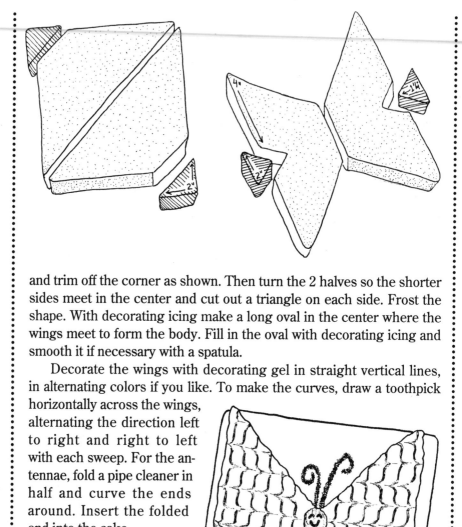

and trim off the corner as shown. Then turn the 2 halves so the shorter sides meet in the center and cut out a triangle on each side. Frost the shape. With decorating icing make a long oval in the center where the wings meet to form the body. Fill in the oval with decorating icing and smooth it if necessary with a spatula.

Decorate the wings with decorating gel in straight vertical lines, in alternating colors if you like. To make the curves, draw a toothpick horizontally across the wings, alternating the direction left to right and right to left with each sweep. For the antennae, fold a pipe cleaner in half and curve the ends around. Insert the folded end into the cake.

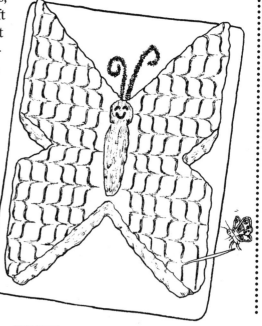

Tip

✔ If you want to write birthday greetings on the Butterfly Cake, outline the butterfly shape with decorating gel in 1 color and then write your message on the wings in a second color.

SAIL AROUND THE WORLD

*C*hildren love the idea of traveling to foreign countries. Having a party that takes an imaginary sail around the world is fun and can even be educational. This can be a costume party. Ask the children to come dressed as one of their ancestors or in the native costume of a country they have visited and to wear any authentic clothing they may have. You may want to have a few items on hand for any children who do not come in costume. Ask friends and neighbors if you can borrow wooden shoes from Holland, a sombrero from Mexico, a kimono from Japan.

For decorations put up travel posters, the more exotic the better, from your local travel agency. Hang up a large map of the world and when the children arrive have them put pushpins or stickers on the countries their family came from or they have visited.

For invitations, make your own postcards from foreign countries. The children can make an album of their "trip" using pictures of themselves taken with an instant camera and photographs from magazines and travel brochures. Make sure you have lots of instant film on hand.

For refreshments, serve appetizers from many different cultures. Check the frozen food section of your grocery store for miniature-size tacos and burritos, egg rolls, pirogi, blini, and bagels. And you can make any of your favorite ethnic foods. Of course, you'll want to have lots of miniature pizzas on hand for those children who are not adventurous eaters. For dessert there is a wonderful Sailboat Cake.

For party favors, give each child a small atlas, imported candy from several different countries, and their handmade photo album.

The Invitation

What you need:
Poster paper
Travel magazines and brochures
Glue stick
Felt-tipped marker
Scissors

To make your own foreign postcards cut pictures from travel magazines and glue them to a 5½ x 3½-inch piece of poster paper. With marker write "Paris" on a photograph of the Eiffel Tower, "Holland" on a picture of tulips in bloom, "Japan" on a picture of Mount Fuji, "Ireland" on a photograph of sheep grazing on a hillside, and so on. On the other side of the postcard draw a line down the middle. On the right side write the child's name and address and place a stamp in the upper right corner. On the left side write "Come Sail Around the World" and include the party information.

Games

Hello-Hola Make a list of "hello" or "good day" in several languages and a list of the languages. See if the children can match the word to the language.

Hola	Spanish
Bon jour	French
Konnichiwa	Japanese
Guten tag	German
Ciao	Italian
Zdrahstvooite	Russian
Bom dia	Portuguese
Annyong ha se yo	Korean
God dag	Swedish

Songs Most children know "Frere Jacques," but you could teach them "Feliz Navidad" and any other simple foreign-language songs you know.

Memory Place 10 or 12 small items on a tray. Have the children look over the tray for 2 minutes, then take it away and ask the children to write down a list of the items. Use small things like chopsticks, a small bottle of perfume, a fan, a foreign coin or stamp, or an old passport.

Capital Idea Write the names of countries on separate 3 x 5 cards or on pieces of construction paper. Do the same with the countries' capital cities and place all the papers around the room. Ask the children to match a country and its capital by picking up the appropriate papers.

A Sailing Ship One child is the ship's captain. He calls out a letter of the alphabet and asks questions that the children try to answer with a word that starts with that letter. For example, the captain calls out "*S*" and then asks, "Where is your ship sailing?" (Sweden, Scandinavia, Southeast Asia.) "From what port did your ship come?" (Savannah, Singapore, San Diego.) "Who is your captain?" (Steven, Susanna, Sally.) "What does your ship carry?" (Shoes, skates, sisters.) "What is your crew's favorite food?" (Shrimp, squash, sandwiches.) Give each child a chance to be the captain and call out another letter of the alphabet.

Photo Album

What you need:
Construction paper
Instant photographs
Travel magazines and
   brochures
Glue and clear tape
Felt-tipped markers
Brass fasteners
Hole punch
Several scissors

Take an instant picture of each child in costume and take lots of pictures of the children while they are playing games. To make the album, have each child place a sheet of colored construction paper on top of and beneath 3 or 4 black sheets. On the left side punch 3 holes through all the layers. Put brass fasteners through the holes. Have the children decorate the front of the album with their name and photograph, then tape or glue pictures cut out from the magazines and brochures and the instant photographs to the black pages.

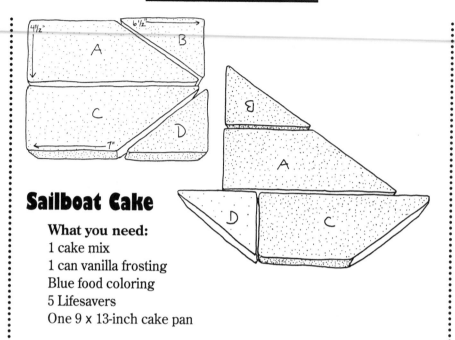

Sailboat Cake

What you need:
1 cake mix
1 can vanilla frosting
Blue food coloring
5 Lifesavers
One 9 x 13-inch cake pan

Bake the cake following package directions. When it is cool, level it and cut it, following the diagram. Arrange the pieces to form a boat. The finished cake measures almost 14 x 18 inches. Frost the sail first. Set aside about 1 tablespoon of the white frosting to use later for any touch-ups. Add food coloring to the rest of the frosting and frost the boat. Put the Lifesavers into the frosting along the top edge of the boat. Put the remainder of the colored frosting into a small plastic bag and cut off one corner. Write birthday greetings on the sail.

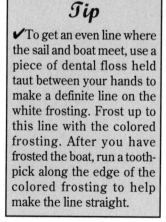

Tip

✔To get an even line where the sail and boat meet, use a piece of dental floss held taut between your hands to make a definite line on the white frosting. Frost up to this line with the colored frosting. After you have frosted the boat, run a toothpick along the edge of the colored frosting to help make the line straight.

PARTIES
for
Children
AGES
10 TO 12

1950s Sock Hop
Beauty Parlor Party
Big Band Concert
Orchestra Concert
Choral Concert
A Farewell Party
Come Fly a Kite Party
Sleepover Secrets
A Pool Party
A Kiddie Pool Party
Opening Night Party
Superbowl Party
A Soda Fountain Party

1950s SOCK HOP

*F*or a 1950s Sock Hop, ask the children to come to the party dressed in '50s clothing. You could suggest poodle skirts or plaid pleated skirts, twin sweater sets and bobby socks for the girls, and chino pants and varsity sweaters for the boys.

For decorations, make posters with pictures cut from magazines of items from the 1950s such as a jukebox, a 1957 Chevy or other '50s car, the Mousketeers, people wearing 1950s clothing, and famous sports players or teams such as the Brooklyn Dodgers. Glue the pictures onto construction paper. Make paper records—cut a 9-inch circle from black construction paper and a 3-inch circle of colored paper for the label—and write the names of rock 'n' roll artists of the '50s such as Bill Haley and the Comets, the Platters, Buddy Holly, Frankie Lymon, the Four Freshmen, the Everly Brothers, and Dion and the Belmonts on the labels. Hang the records and the posters on the wall and add crepe paper streamers.

Borrow records from the 1950s if you know someone who has a collection or get cassettes of the music. Teach the children the Lindy Hop, the Stroll, the Twist, and other dances of the 1950s and '60s. For refreshments have big bowls of potato chips and dip, pretzels, and popcorn with lots of soda to drink. Serve the Greatest Hits Cake when the dancing is done. For favors give each child individual-size servings of candy that was popular in the 1950s such as Good & Plenty, Raisinets, Dots, Goldenberg's Peanut Chews, and Jujyfruits.

The Invitation

What you need:
Construction paper
Felt-tipped markers
Pencil
Glue stick
Protractor
Scissors

Cut an 8-inch circle from black construction paper and fold it in half. For the record label, glue a 3½-inch half-circle of colored construction paper to the center along the fold. For the party information, glue a 6-inch circle of white or light-colored construction paper to the inside of the card.

On the outside of the card use a protractor and a pencil to draw concentric lines that look like record groves. Place the point of the protractor on the center of the fold and draw a half-circle every ⅛ inch from the outside edge of the record in to the label. With a black marker draw a small half-circle in the center of the label to look like the hole in the record. With a colored marker write "Mike's Sock Hop" on the label and write the party information on the inside. Ask the guests to come dressed in 1950s clothing.

Games

Famous Couples of the '50s Write the names of famous couples separately on self-sticking labels. When the children arrive, give them each a name to wear and ask them to find the other half of the couple. If you have an odd number of guests, use a trio of names such as Kukla, Fran and Ollie. You can use couples like:

    Lucille Ball and Desi Arnaz
    Elizabeth Taylor and Mike Todd
    The Lone Ranger and Tonto
    Our Miss Brooks and Walter Denton
    Wally Cleaver and Beaver
    Howdy Doody and Princess Summer Fall Winter Spring
    Matt Dillon and Miss Kitty

Back-to-Back Relay Race Divide the children into 2 teams and have them choose a partner. Each couple stands back-to-back with arms linked and runs sideways to a goal line and back. The first team to finish wins.

Bowling Arrange ten 1-liter plastic soda bottles in a triangle with the point facing the children. Each child in turn gets 3 chances to roll a ball and knock down the pins. Score like regular bowling.

Guess What Gather a list of advertising slogans from the 1950s and 1960s that were used in television, radio, and magazines. Give the children the list and see if they can match the slogan to the product. Here are a few to get you started.

"See the U.S.A. in a . . ."	Chevrolet
"Look sharp, feel sharp, be sharp."	Gillette Blue Blade razor
"Brush-a, brush-a, brush-a with the new . . ."	Ipana toothpaste
"Clings like cloth."	Kleenex table napkins
"Hunts them down like radar."	Raid
"That foaming cleanser."	Ajax
"A little dab will do ya . . ."	Brylcreem

Dance Contest Give a prize to the person who does the wildest Twist, to the couple who have the most innovative moves in the Lindy Hop, to the couple who perform the smoothest Stroll.

Greatest Hits Cake

What you need:
1 cake mix
1 can dark chocolate frosting
Two 9-inch round cake pans
A new wide-tooth comb
Construction paper
Wax paper
Glue stick
Black felt-tipped marker
Compass
Scissors

Bake the cake following package directions. One cake mix will make 2 record cakes. Frost each layer separately. To simulate the record groves, gently press the comb into the frosting as you circle the top of the cake with it. Make grooves around the side of the cake the same way.

To make the label, using a compass cut a 3½-inch circle from con-

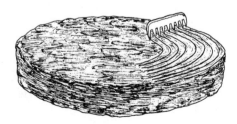
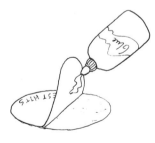

struction paper and from wax paper. Glue them together with glue stick. With the marker, write "Happy Birthday" and "Greatest Hits" around the edge of the label and "Mike" in the middle. Color in a small circle at the very center to represent the hole in the record. Place the label in the center of the cake.

BEAUTY PARLOR PARTY

*I*f your daughter loves to try out new hairdos, you can create a beauty parlor in your home where she and her friends can have their hair styled and get a manicure. To help with the hairdos ask a friend who is adept at hairstyling, a teenager or two who know the latest styles, or hire a local beautician to create a hairstyle for each of the girls. Because each hairstyle takes time, this party will work best with no more than 5 or 6 guests. For the hairdos, you will need a bag of combs so each girl can have her own comb, a curling iron, mousse or gel, hair spray, bobby pins, hairpins, and ponytail holders.

You can hire a teenage girl to give a manicure to each girl or let the girls polish each other's nails. Set them up in a quiet corner and put a piece of plastic on the floor to make cleanup easier.

While one girl is having her hair done, the other girls can make a barrette and have a manicure. Take an instant photograph of each girl in her new hairdo, and for favors put the photograph along with a comb, brush, and hand mirror in a clear plastic cosmetics case. The girls will also take home their handmade barrette.

The Invitation

What you need:
Construction paper
Small plastic barrettes
4-inch paper doilies
Glue stick
Felt-tipped markers
Scissors

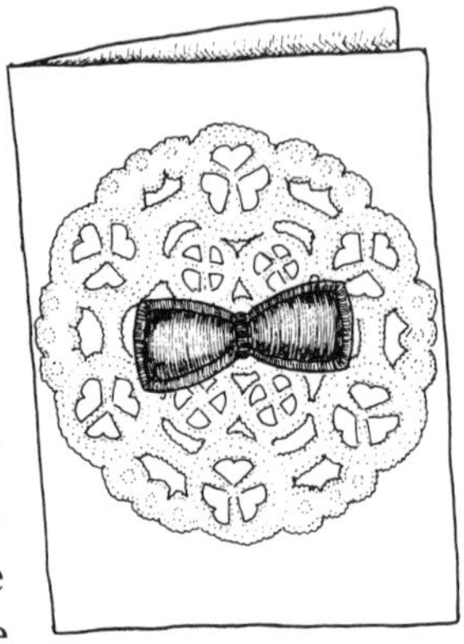

Cut a 5 x 8-inch piece of construction paper and fold it in half so you have a 5 x 4-inch card. Place the plastic barrette on the doily to see where the barrette ends lie. Cut out the 2 motifs on the doily that are under the barrette ends. Attach the barrette to the doily through the 2 holes and glue the outer edge of the doily to the front of the card. By keeping the glue away from the barrette you will enable the person who receives the invitation to remove the barrette and use it. Write the party information on the inside.

Bow Barrette

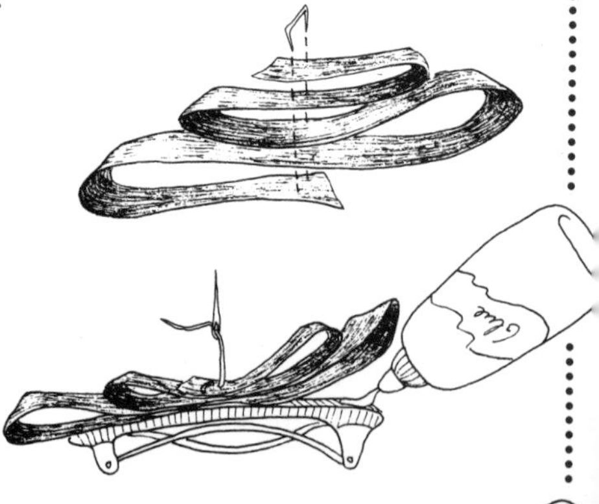

What you need:
3-inch long barrette backings
18-inch length of ½-inch
   or ⅝-inch wide fabric ribbon
Rosettes
Needle and sewing thread
Glue
Stapler

Fold the ribbon into a bow as shown in the diagram, making the first loops slightly longer than the barrette. Staple the bow in the center and glue it to the barrette backing. With needle and thread sew the bow to the barrette, stitching in the center of the bow only. Glue a rosette on top of the bow, covering the sewing stitches. Allow the glue to dry.

Hairdo Cake and Cupcakes

What you need:
1 cake mix
1 can frosting
2 ounces coconut
Food coloring
Tubes of decorating gel: brown, yellow, and red
Tubes of decorating icing
1 licorice shoelace (optional)
Assorted cake decorations
Small round candies for the barrettes
One 9-inch round cake pan
Cupcake pans
Paper cupcake liners
Toothpicks

Mix the cake following the package directions and bake it in 1 round layer and 12 cupcakes. When they are cool, frost the cake and cupcakes.

Add food coloring to the coconut to make it blond, red, brown, or black to match the birthday girl's hair color. Arrange the coconut on the cake so it looks like hair. With a toothpick draw eyes, nose, and mouth, then draw them with decorating gel and decorating icing. Cut small pieces of licorice for the eyelashes. Add cake decorations for the eyes and candy for the barrettes.

With a variety of decorating icing and gel, decorate the cupcakes so they resemble the party guests. Add cake decorations for the eyes and nose.

Tip

✔The amount of cake batter from a cake mix or recipe for a 2-layer cake is somewhat flexible. You can make fewer than 12 cupcakes or even a couple more and there will still be enough batter for a 9-inch round layer.

BIG BAND CONCERT

*M*usic is a wonderful part of a child's life. If your child plays a musical instrument, you can create a party around his musical ability. For decorations hang musical posters on the walls along with large musical notes cut from black construction paper. For the posters, ask at your local concert hall or a record store, or borrow them from a teenage friend who collects them.

Ask the guests to bring their own instruments to the party. For those children who don't play, have on hand some children's instruments such as handbells, maracas, tambourines, kazoos, and make-your-own drums (large coffee cans and wooden spoons). Also have sheet music for "Happy Birthday" and several other of your child's favorite songs. The children can practice a song or two to perform and then all of the guests can serenade the birthday child with "Happy Birthday."

The Invitation

What you need:
White construction paper,
    8 x 8½ inches
Black construction paper,
    2½ x 3 inches
Black thin-line felt-tipped
    marker
Glue
Pencil and scissors

Fold the white construction paper in half. With a pencil, starting at the right side, draw 8 lines 1 inch apart. Trace over the lines with black marker. For the black keys, cut six ½ x 2½-inch strips of black construction paper. Center and glue them over the marker lines, following the drawing for placement. On the inside write "You are invited to a Big Band Concert," give the party time and place, and ask the guests to bring their own musical instruments.

Piano Cake

What you need:
1 cake mix
1 can vanilla frosting
Two 36-inch long licorice
   shoelaces
One 5-ounce package (of 10)
   licorice twists
One 9 x 13-inch cake pan
1 piece white construction paper
Felt-tipped marker
Ruler

Bake the cake following package directions. Allow it to cool and cut it in half lengthwise. Arrange the 2 long pieces short sides together and frost the entire shape. The cake will be about 4¼ x 25 inches.

Cut the licorice shoelaces into seventeen 1⅜-inch pieces and seven 4-inch pieces. Cut the licorice twists into seventeen 3-inch pieces.

Measuring with the ruler as explained in the box, draw 24 lines 1 inch apart along the entire cake. Starting at the right side of the cake, center a licorice twist on the line and place a small piece of licorice shoelace below it. On the next line place a 4-inch length of licorice shoelace. Continue forming the keys, using the lico-

> ### Tip
> ✔To help you mark the placement of the keys on the cake, place a ruler or yardstick parallel to the cake. Insert a toothpick into the cake at each inch mark. Use dental floss held taut between your hands to lightly press a line on the cake at each toothpick.

rice twists for the black keys and the licorice shoelaces for the outline of the white keys, as illustrated.

For the greetings, fold the construction paper in half and open it up. With a felt-tipped marker draw a G clef and staff as shown and write your birthday greetings. Stand the paper up behind the cake like sheet music.

Orchestra Concert

If your child plays a stringed instrument, you can invite guests to an Orchestra Concert. Decorate the party room with posters of orchestras and famous conductors.

Choral Concert

If your child loves to sing, plan a Choral Concert. Decorate the walls with posters of famous singers. Have enough sheet music and lyrics to songs so there is 1 for every 2 children. Have the children make up their own lyrics to popular songs based on their own experiences in school.

A FAREWELL PARTY

*I*f a child in your neighborhood is moving away you can have a farewell party in his or her honor. Send an invitation in the shape of a house with a child's face looking out of an open window. In the invitation ask each guest to write down their favorite characteristic of the guest of honor or their fondest memory of the child and bring this to the party.

At the party the children can create a book of memories for the person who is leaving and make their own stationery so they can write to him or her. Buy small address books and put one child's name on each book. During the party have the children put their names and addresses in all the books but their own. Make sure the party child writes his or her new address in all the books too.

When the projects are complete, serve the New House Cake. For favors give the children a pen or a decorative pencil and some stamps to take home along with their stationery and the address book filled with the names and addresses of their friends. The child who is moving away will also have a memory book to take along to the new house as a reminder of the friends left behind.

The Invitation

What you need:
Construction paper:
  yellow, brown, red,
  and white
Glue stick
Felt-tipped markers
Scissors and razor
  (optional)

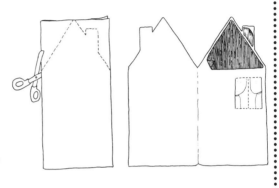

Cut an 8 x 8½-inch piece of yellow construction paper and fold it in half. Cut the top end to a point with a chimney as shown in the diagram. Cut a triangle of brown for the roof, a red rectangle for the chimney, and a white rectangle for the door and glue these onto the house. Draw two 1¼ x 1½-inch rectangles for the upper windows. With felt-tipped markers outline the door and windows and add curtains, doorknob, and door trim. With scissors or a razor carefully cut the top, bottom, and down the center of the upper right window. Fold back the flaps and draw a child's face inside the window on the inside of the invitation. Write the party information on the inside and ask the children to write about a favorite moment with the child who is moving away. The children should write on a standard 8½ x 11-inch piece of typing paper, sign the paper, and bring it with them to the party.

Stationery

What you need:
Typing paper
Legal-size envelopes
Ink pads in 2 or more
    colors
A new sponge
New pencils
Scissors

The children can trans-
form white typing paper and
standard envelopes into their own
personal stationery. Or if you can purchase paper by the pound, you can buy
stationery and envelopes in a variety of colors.

To make the shapes for printing, cut the corners off the sponge for triangles, cut squares about ½ to ¾ inch in length, and cut ¼-inch-wide strips. Use the pencil erasers to make circles. Have the children press the shapes and erasers into the ink pads and then onto the paper in any arrangement they like. They can decorate the paper and make a coordinating design on the envelopes.

Memory Book

What you need:
Refill package of self-stick pages for a photograph album
Construction paper
Ribbon
Instant camera and film

Before the party, have your child make a cover for the album by writing "Brian's Book of Memories" on a piece of construction paper. Insert this under the plastic of the first album page. Put the pages together and bind the book by tying ribbon through the holes.

During the party, have someone take pictures of each child, of the children in small groups, and the children with the guest of honor. To make the book, put each child's written memory on the right side of a photograph album page and pictures of that child and the guest of honor on the left-hand page. If you have lots of photographs, you can arrange some of them on additional self-stick pages at the end of the book, and also give out some of them to the children as they leave.

New House Cake

What you need:
2 pound cakes
1 can vanilla frosting
1 tube decorating gel
1 tube white decorating icing
1 box miniature butter cookies or
   crackers
1 licorice shoelace
Green mint leaves and green gumdrops
Chiclets or colored gum squares

To make the house, follow the directions for constructing the Hansel and Gretel Cottage on page 43. Cover the roof with the cookies or crackers. Cut short lengths of the licorice shoelace to outline the front door and windows. Make window curtains with decorating gel. Place mint leaves and gumdrops in front of the house for bushes. With decorating icing make a front pathway and fill it in with Chiclets. Make a window on the door and the door handle with decorating gel.

> ## *Tips*
>
> ✔If you do not have candy on hand for this cake, draw the door and window frames with a dark color decorating gel and make the trees and bushes with green decorating icing. Outline the front pathway with green decorating icing and fill in the center with white frosting.
>
> ✔To make a red tiled roof, use only red Chiclets or other coated gum squares.

COME FLY A KITE PARTY

*F*lying a kite is such fun for kids of all ages that the parents will be as enthusiastic about this party as the children. This is a great party for active children because they can make a kite and then fly it. And what a feeling of exhilaration, that moment when you actually get the kite in the air.

In addition to the supplies needed to make the kites you will need to purchase enough kite string so all the children can fly their kites. You may want to serve the Kite Cake after the children have completed making their kites but before they go outside to fly them. The children will be taking their kites home so you may want to make the favors as simple as a glider kit and some candy.

The Invitation

What you need:
Construction paper:
  blue, white, green,
  and yellow for each
  invitation
String, about 5 inches
Felt-tipped markers
Glue stick
Scissors

Cut an 8 x 8½-inch piece of blue construction paper and fold it in half. Cut a 4 x 7-inch piece of white construction paper and glue it to the front of the card. Starting at the top left side of the card, draw 3 curves that look like 3 overlapping clouds. Open up the card and cut along these curves, cutting through the white and blue paper on the front only. On the blue paper that forms the back of the card, round off the top corners.

For mountains, cut out 3 green triangles about 3 inches high and glue them to the bottom of the card. From yellow paper cut a kite about 1¾ x ⅞ inches and draw the dowels with marker. Glue the string to the bottom of the kite and glue the kite to the blue paper but keep the kite string in front of the clouds. On the inside write "Come fly a kite" and include the party information.

A Sled Kite

What you need:
1 large heavy-duty plastic garbage bag for each kite
Two ⅜-inch dowels, each 16 inches long
Toothpicks
Crepe paper streamers
   for the tails
String
Felt-tipped markers
Clear tape
Scissors

Draw a 16 x 20-inch rectangle on the garbage bag. Make a mark 4 inches in from either side on the top and bottom, and make a mark 6 inches down from the top on both sides. Connect these 6 marks for the kite shape. With markers, draw a design on the shape. Cut out the kite. Turn the kite over and place the dowels on it so they are parallel to each

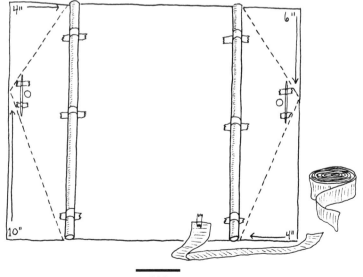

other. Tape them in place using several pieces of tape for each dowel. To prevent the string from ripping the kite when it is flying, tape a toothpick ½-inch in from each side point. With the point of the scissors, make a hole just inside the toothpick. For tails, cut 3 or 4 pieces of crepe paper streamers and tape them to the bottom edge of the kite. Tie the ends of a 40-inch piece of string through each side hole. Attach the flying string by tying a loop around the 40-inch string.

Kite Cake

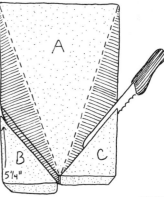

What you need:
1 cake mix
1 can frosting
2 tubes decorating gel
One 9 x 13-inch cake pan
Crepe paper streamer, 2 feet long

Bake the cake following package directions and allow it to cool. Cut the cake as shown, arrange the pieces to form a kite, and frost the shape. With one color decorating gel, write "Happy Birthday." With the other gel, draw lines where the dowels would be, starting at the outside edges and going in toward the writing. Cut the crepe paper streamer into one 18-inch length and two 3-inch lengths. Tie the smaller pieces around the longer one as you would on a kite streamer. At the bottom point of the kite, make a small cut in the cake and insert one end of the crepe paper streamer into the cake.

SLEEPOVER SECRETS

*G*irls love sharing secrets with their very best friends, and having a sleepover party means they can giggle and gossip long into the night. You can invite the girls for early evening and show them how to make their own diary, a fabric-covered cardboard book with typing-paper pages, for keeping secrets and personal thoughts. When they finish making the diaries, surprise them with the Ice-Cream Cake.

For party favors have a grab bag. Cover an open cardboard carton with gift-wrapping paper so it looks like a gift box. Fill it with an assortment of small items: colorful note pads, interesting pens and pencils, small address books, high-bouncing balls, plastic bracelets, and stickers. Have the girls take turns reaching into the box to grab a party favor until all the favors have been claimed. Rent a favorite video, or the newest release if it is appropriate for their age, so the girls can have a quiet activity before trying to settle down for the night. A promise of pancakes for breakfast may induce some of them to drift off to sleep.

The Invitation

What you need:
Construction paper: white, black, pink, and yellow
Glue
Ruler
Scissors

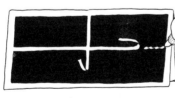

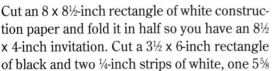

Cut an 8 x 8½-inch rectangle of white construction paper and fold it in half so you have an 8½ x 4-inch invitation. Cut a 3½ x 6-inch rectangle of black and two ¼-inch strips of white, one 5⅝ inches and one 3½ inches long. Glue the black rectangle to the center of the invitation, then glue the white strips, the window mullions, on top of

the black. Using the pattern as a guide, cut 1 window curtain from pink paper. Turn it over so you have the mirror image and cut out another. Glue the curtains to the left and right sides of the window. Draw a moon on yellow paper, cut it out, and glue it to the upper right window pane. On the inside write "Share your secrets at Jessica's Sleepover Party" and include the party date and time.

Personal Diary

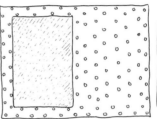

What you need for each diary:

Fabric, about 11 x 15 inches

Two 6 x 9-inch pieces of cardboard

12 sheets of typing paper

White glue

Needle and white thread

Place the fabric face down on the table. Spread glue evenly on both pieces of cardboard. Place them glued side down on the fabric, leaving ¼ inch between them for the book's spine and about 1 inch of fabric all around the edges. Put a line of glue around the outside edges of the cardboard but not along the spine. Fold the excess fabric over the 2 long sides first. Put a lot of glue on the corners. Tuck in the excess fabric and fold in the fabric on the sides.

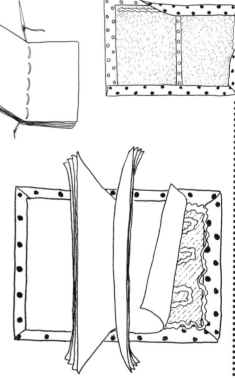

To make the pages, hold the 12 typing paper pages together and fold them in half. Thread the needle and make a knot in the end of the thread. Stitch the pages together along the fold, leaving both the beginning and end knots on the outside. Place the pages on top of the cover with the stitching lying along the spine. Glue the first page to the inside front cover and the last page to the inside back cover.

Ice-Cream Cake

What you need:
3 quarts ice cream, different flavors
2 packages (about 9 ounces each) chocolate wafer cookies
2 tablespoons margarine
1 tube decorating gel
One 9 or 10-inch springform cake pan
Plastic wrap

Preheat the oven to 350°F.
Crumble 20 to 25 chocolate cookies
by placing them in a plastic bag and pressing on them with a rolling pin. Melt the margarine and mix the margarine and cookie crumbs in a small bowl. Press the mixture into the bottom of the springform pan. Bake for 10 minutes. Set the pan aside and allow it to cool thoroughly, then put it in the refrigerator.

Crumble about 15 cookies but keep the pieces large. Let the first quart of ice cream soften slightly. Spread the ice cream on top of the cookie crust. Sprinke the cookie crumbs on top of the ice cream and top with a piece of plastic wrap. Put in the freezer and freeze for 1 hour.

Crumble about 15 cookies and let the second quart of ice cream soften slightly. Remove the plastic wrap and make a second layer of ice cream and cookie crumbs the same as the first. Cover with plastic wrap and freeze for 1 hour.

> ## Tip
>
> ✔To make the ice cream easier to spread into a layer, allow it to soften slightly, then use a large bread knife to cut it into slices ¾- to 1-inch thick. Place the slices close together on top of the cookie crust and then use a large spoon to smooth the slices into 1 layer.

Let the third quart of ice cream soften slightly. Remove the plastic wrap from the cake pan and make a third layer of ice cream only. Cover with plastic wrap and put in the freezer overnight.

Crumble about 5 cookies for the top of the cake. Take the cake out of the freezer just before you plan to serve it. Dip a butter knife in hot water and run it along the edge of the cake be-tween the cake and the pan. Then remove the sides of the pan. Sprinkle the cookie crumbs around the perimeter of the cake and write the birth-day greetings with decorating gel.

A POOL PARTY

Celebrate summer or a summer birthday by having a party around the pool. You can get everyone in the mood for outdoor fun and games by sending out invitations in the shape of sequined sunglasses.

Depending on the number of guests you invite, you'll want to invite at least 2 adults who are good swimmers to act as lifeguards. These peo-ple are not to help set up the party but are to keep their eyes on the pool while any children are swimming.

Plan some games to play in the water but also allow time for the chil-dren to swim and play in the water on their own. You don't want too much structure at a pool party, but do emphasize basic water safety rules. A nice idea for those children who do not want to spend the entire time in the pool: set up a croquet game on the lawn and have quiet games like checkers or chess on the patio.

While the children are playing, set up a buffet of bread, rolls, sliced meat, and cheese so the children can make their own sandwiches. For dessert serve Ice-Cream Cone Cupcakes, the kind that won't melt in the sun.

For favors give each child an individual-size shopping bag containing a pair of sunglasses, a trial-size tube of sunscreen lotion, and a comic book.

The Invitation

What you need:
Construction paper, 12 x 18 inches
Black construction paper
White glue
Sequins
Felt-tipped marker
Scissors

To draw a pair of sunglasses on the construction paper, make two 2½-inch circles about ¼ inch apart. Then draw a 5-inch-long earpiece out from each circle. For lenses cut two 1½-inch circles from black construction paper and glue them to the glasses. Fold the earpieces where the hinges would be. Glue sequins around the frames. Turn the glasses over and write the party information on the back. You can ask each child to bring a towel, to save yourself some laundry. But have towels on hand for those children who do not remember to bring one.

If you do not have the large-size construction paper, you can make the glasses from 9 x 12-inch paper. The front of the glasses and one earpiece will fit on the paper; draw the second earpiece below the first. Cut out the pieces and tape them together.

Games

Water Volleyball Use a net, put a length of clothesline cord across the center of the pool and anchor it on either side. Divide the children into 2 teams and give them a beach ball to volley across the rope.

Pool Polo Establish a goal at either end of the pool. Divide the children into 2 teams facing each other. The object of the game is to get a beach ball to the opponent's end of the pool to score a goal. The children can hit the ball but not throw it.

Sailboat Race Divide the children into 3 or more teams. Give each team a child's plastic sailboat. The children work together as a team to get the sailboat to the other end of the pool without touching it. They may splash the water around the boat or blow on it but they may not touch it. The first team to get the boat to the other end of the pool wins.

The Hokey Pokey Sing and dance the Hokey Pokey in the middle of the pool. At first most kids will think this is silly, but they will soon discover it's a lot of fun.

Ice-Cream Cone Cupcakes

What you need:
1 cake mix
1 can frosting
Flat-bottomed
    ice-cream cones
Sprinkles
Cupcake pans

Mix the cake following the package directions. Stand the ice-cream cones in the cupcake pans and fill the cones one-half to two-thirds full. Bake following the package directions for cupcakes. When they are cool, frost them. Pour the sprinkles onto a flat plate and dip the cupcakes into them. Makes 24 to 30 cupcakes.

Tip

✔Do not fill the ice-cream cones more than two-thirds full or the batter will ooze over the side of the cones before they bake.

A Kiddie Pool Party

You can have a wonderful fun-filled party for young children around an inflatable kiddie pool. Set up a lawn sprinkler so the children can run and play between the pool and the sprinkler. For favors, at the beginning of the party, give each child a plastic pail and shovel so they can play with them in the water. Before the party begins, write each child's name on the pail with a permanent felt-tipped marker.

Invite the parents to come too, so the children have someone to watch over them and help them dry off. Make a tray of sandwiches and a pitcher of lemonade before the party begins so you are free to enjoy the fun. You can serve lunch and the Ice-Cream Cone Cupcakes around the pool.

OPENING NIGHT PARTY

*C*elebrate the opening night of a class play by inviting everyone—actors, director, and stagehands—to your house for a congratulatory party.

To decorate, make a poster of praise. Cut out words of praise like "brilliant" and "enthralling" from newspaper and magazine advertisements for movies and plays and if necessary enlarge them at your local copy center. At the top of the poster write "The Elm Street School presents *Harvey*," and then "The critics rave." Paste the words from the magazines and newspapers on the poster. Hang the poster on the wall and surround it with a border of crepe paper streamers. Blow up balloons and with a felt-tipped marker, write the name of a character in the play on each balloon, and hang the balloons around the room.

Depending on the time of the party, you

"★★★★!"

"WONDERFUL!"

"Non-stop fun!"

"WOW!"

"TWO THUMBS UP!"

"YOU'LL LOVE IT"

"FANTASTIC!"

may want to serve a light meal like pizza or sandwiches or you may just serve the Bouquet of Balloons Cake and soda.

The Invitation

What you need:
White construction paper
Newspaper and magazine advertisements
Black felt-tipped marker
Glue stick
Scissors

Cut an 8 x 8½-inch piece of construction paper and fold it in half. Cut out congratulatory words like "good job," "well done," "awesome," and "enchanting" from the newspaper and magazine advertisements for movies and plays and glue them onto the construction paper. Or you can write your own words using different lettering styles. Or, if you have a computer, you can print the words in different typefaces. On the inside of the invitation write "Opening Night Party. The Elm Street School presents *Harvey*. Come celebrate." Also include the date, place, and time of the party.

Games

Twenty Questions On separate pieces of paper write down the names of the play's characters as well as the director, stage designer, and other crew members. Have each child choose one. The other children ask questions about the character that can be answered with a yes or no. If no one guesses who the character is after 20 questions, the child reveals the identity.

Detective Ask the children to look around the room and then to cover their eyes. Remove an object. Have the children look again and see if they can guess what is missing. The person who guesses correctly gets to remove the next object.

Seven Up Have half the children cover their eyes. The other half tiptoe around quietly and tap 1 child gently. When all the tappers are finished and back in their places, the other children look up and try to guess who tapped them. If a correct, that child and the tapper trade places.

Bouquet of Balloons Cake

What you need:
1 cake mix
1 can vanilla frosting
Food coloring
1 tube decorating gel
One 9 x 13-inch cake pan
1 cupcake pan
2 yards ¼-inch wide ribbon
Scissors

Mix the cake following package directions. Make 6 cupcakes, filling each one more than three-quarters full. Put the remaining batter in the 9 x 13-inch pan. Bake according to package directions for the cupcakes; bake the cake about 5 minutes less than the suggested time. Allow to cool.

Put 6 generous tablespoons of frosting in 6 small bowls. Frost the cake with the remaining frosting. Add a different food coloring to each of the 6 bowls. Cut off the rounded top of each cupcake and frost it with 1 of the colors of frosting. Place the cupcake tops on the cake.

For the balloon strings, cut the ribbon into five 12-inch lengths, one 2-inch length, and one 10-inch length. Place the 2-inch ribbon between the top cupcake and the one right below it. Then place 1 end of each of the 5 same-size ribbons under the other 5 cupcakes, letting the ribbons lie on the cake. Gather the ribbons together at the bottom of the cake. Tie a bow around them with the 10-inch ribbon. With decorating gel write "Bravo!" to the left of the ribbons.

SUPERBOWL PARTY

*S*uperbowl Sunday is a perfect day for a party for football lovers. You can generate some team spirit by decorating the room with crepe paper streamers and pennants in your favorite team's colors. Cut pennants from construction paper in the appropriate colors, write the team's name on them, and glue them to drinking straws. You can hang these on the wall or give one to each guest.

Ask the guests to arrive about one half hour before kickoff and start the festivities by asking everyone to predict the score after each quarter of play. Have bowls of potato chips and raw vegetables and dip for munching during the game. Set up a buffet table with hero sandwiches—Italian bread filled with sliced meat and cheese—cut into manageable-size pieces, and cole slaw and potato salad. The Football Field Cake can be the centerpiece of the table.

You can plan a few games to play during halftime, but remember that some people will want to watch the halftime show and others will spend this time socializing.

The Invitation

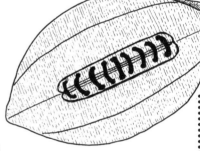

What you need:
Brown construction paper
Black felt-tipped marker
Scissors

Cut an 8 x 8½-inch piece of construction paper and fold it in half. To make a football shape, use a plate with a 7- to 8-inch diameter. With the fold on top, place the plate on the fold and trace around it. Move the plate to the cut edges and trace it again. Cut away the excess paper. With marker draw the football's seams and stitching, and write the party information on the inside.

Games

Guess the Score Label 4 pieces of paper "first quarter," "halftime," "third quarter," and "final score." Ask each guest to predict the score and write it on the appropriate paper. At the end of each quarter award a prize, such as a small bag of miniature chocolate footballs, to the person who has come closest to guessing the correct score.

Celebrities Buy a copy of a weekly gossip magazine and a sports magazine. Cut out photographs of celebrities—pop stars, ball players, television and film stars—and glue them to a posterboard. Number the photographs and have each guest guess the identities. At halftime, read the answers and award a prize to the person who got the most correct.

Hum That Tune If someone is musical, ask them to hum or sing, without using identifiable words, the jingles from television commercials. See if the guests can guess the products. This is a group effort so there is no need for prizes.

Football Field Cake

What you need:
1 cake mix
1 can frosting
3 ounces coconut
Green food coloring
1 tube white decorating icing
3 licorice shoelaces
4 peppermint sticks
2 sugar wafer cookies
One 9 x 13-inch cake pan
Brown and white construction paper
Toothpicks

Bake the cake following package directions. While the cake is cooling, tint the coconut green and allow it to dry, and cut nine 8½-inch long pieces of licorice shoelace for the yard lines.

Level the cake. Add several drops of green food coloring to the frosting and frost the entire cake. Put 1 licorice shoelace across the center of the cake, then put 4 more about 1 inch apart on each side. Sprinkle the green coconut on the top of the cake, then gently brush away the coconut that is on top of the licorice yard lines.

Before inserting the peppermint sticks for the goalposts, stick a sharp knife into the end of the cake, making 2 cuts 2 inches apart. Insert the

peppermint sticks
into the cuts. Put 2 lines of
decorating icing on the sugar
wafer cookies and gently press
these lines of icing onto the peppermint sticks. If you glue the cookie to
the peppermint sticks first, the cookie will fall off as you insert the sticks
into the cake.

For the scoreboard, cut a 3 x 8-inch piece
of brown construction paper and a 2¼ x 3¼-
inch piece of white paper. Write "Go Team"
on the white paper. To make the scoreboard,
follow the directions for the soccer field scoreboard on page 81.

> ### Tip
> ✔ If your child has minia-
> ture football player toys,
> you can wash them thor-
> oughly and place them on
> the cake.

A SODA FOUNTAIN PARTY

*F*or your next party set up an old-fashioned soda fountain in your
home. Have the children make their own soda jerk hats and then let them
take over the soda fountain and make treats for everyone. You will need
a variety of flavors of ice cream, syrups, marshmallow fluff, and toppings

like chopped nuts, malt powder, miniature marshmallows, whipped cream, and, of course, maraschino cherries. Have several ice-cream scoops so a number of children can be making sundaes and sodas at the same time.

Take an instant photograph of each child and his or her ice-cream creation and award prizes to the most inventive sundae, the most traditional, the best-looking, the sundae that used the most ingredients, and even to the least appetizing creation. To finish off the party bring out the Ice-Cream Cone Cake.

The Invitation

What you need:
Construction paper in a variety of colors
Brown felt-tipped marker
Hole punch
Glue stick
Scissors
Tweezers (optional)

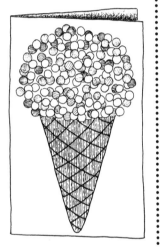

Cut a 6 x 7-inch piece of construction paper and fold it in half to make a 3½ x 6-inch card. For the ice-cream cone, cut a 2¼ x 3½-inch triangle out of brown paper, and round off the point. Make latticelike lines on the cone with a marker and glue the cone to the card. With the hole punch make lots of dots in several different colors. Glue these dots to the card in the shape of a scoop of ice cream. If the dots are difficult to pick up, use a pair of tweezers. Write the party information inside.

Soda Jerk Hat

What you need:
White construction paper
White crepe paper
Clear tape
Scissors

Make a cuff 3 x 24 inches by taping together 2 pieces of construction paper. Adjust it to fit the child's head and tape it closed. Crease the center

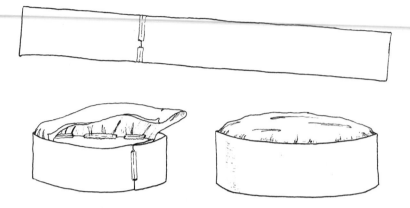

front and center back. Cut an 8 x 12-inch piece of crepe paper and tape the long sides to the inside top of the cuff, easing the excess crepe paper so it fits inside the cuff.

Ice-Cream Sundaes

Here are some suggestions for traditional ice-cream sundaes. Of course some of the children will want to create their own concoctions. And all of them can be topped off with whipped cream and a maraschino cherry.

Brown Cow Chocolate ice cream with marshmallow fluff.

Maple Walnut Sundae Vanilla ice cream topped with maple syrup and chopped walnuts.

Rocky Road Chocolate ice cream with chocolate syrup, marshmallow fluff, and chopped nuts on top.

Dusty Road Chocolate ice cream with chocolate syrup, marshmallow fluff, and malt powder on top.

Heavenly Hash Vanilla ice cream topped with chocolate chips, miniature marshmallows, and chopped nuts.

Mississippi Mud Sundae Put graham cracker crumbs in the bottom of the dish, add chocolate syrup, then ice cream. Top with chocolate syrup and a sprinkling of graham cracker crumbs.

Banana Split On a banana cut in half lengthwise put 1 scoop each of vanilla, chocolate, and strawberry ice cream. Top the vanilla ice cream with chocolate syrup, the chocolate with marshmallow fluff, and the strawberry with crushed pineapple syrup. Top all three with whipped cream, chopped nuts, and maraschino cherries.

Kitchen Sink The soda fountain of my childhood served a gargantuan sundae that served at least 10 people. It contained all kinds of ice cream and syrups and was topped with a mountain of whipped cream. You can make your own version of a Kitchen Sink to use up all the leftover ice cream and syrups from the party.

Ice-Cream Sodas

Milk Shake Put ice cream, syrup, and milk into a blender and blend slightly; the result should contain lumps of ice cream.

Malted Add malt powder to the recipe above.

Root Beer Float Put vanilla ice cream in a glass and pour root beer over it.

Black-and-White Soda Put chocolate syrup in the bottom of a glass, add vanilla ice cream, and pour seltzer over both.

Egg Cream Put chocolate syrup in the bottom of a glass, add a little milk, and mix. Fill the glass with seltzer.

Ice-Cream Cone Cake

What you need:
2 cake mixes
2 cans frosting, 1 vanilla, 1 milk chocolate
2 tubes cake decorating gel, 1 chocolate, 1 a color of your choice
Sprinkles
Two 9-inch round baking pans
One 9 x 13-inch baking pan

Bake the 2 cake mixes according to package directions, making 1 cake in the round pans and 1 in the rectangular pan. When the cakes are cool,

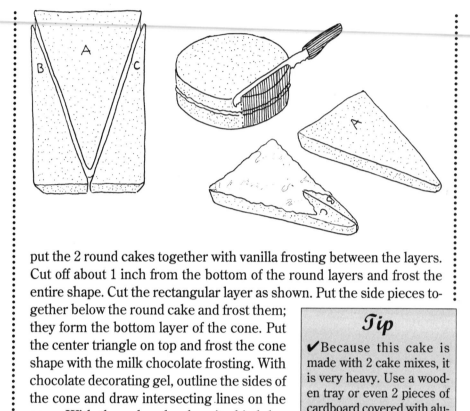

put the 2 round cakes together with vanilla frosting between the layers. Cut off about 1 inch from the bottom of the round layers and frost the entire shape. Cut the rectangular layer as shown. Put the side pieces together below the round cake and frost them; they form the bottom layer of the cone. Put the center triangle on top and frost the cone shape with the milk chocolate frosting. With chocolate decorating gel, outline the sides of the cone and draw intersecting lines on the cone. With the colored gel, write birthday greetings on the ice-cream part of the cake and top with sprinkles.

Tip

✔ Because this cake is made with 2 cake mixes, it is very heavy. Use a wooden tray or even 2 pieces of cardboard covered with aluminum foil as the serving tray.

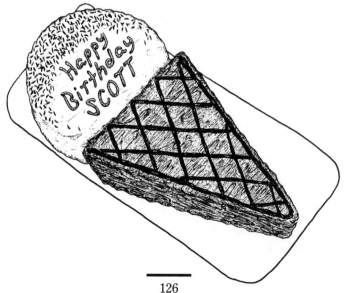

HOLIDAYS
and
FAMILY EVENTS

Christmas

Hanukkah

Valentine's Day

Easter

Passover

Mother's Day

Father's Day

Graduation

Fourth of July

Halloween

Thanksgiving

New Year's Eve

Baby's Christening

Confirmation

Baby's First Birthday

CHRISTMAS

a few days before Christmas is the perfect time to have a tree-trimming party. The children can make a variety of Christmas tree ornaments, some to decorate your tree and some to take home for their own tree. To keep things organized, gather all the materials you will need to make each ornament and put them in separate boxes or shopping bags. Ask an adult or teenager to supervise the making of each ornament. Ornaments are such fun to make that the adults and teenagers will probably want to join in, so have lots of supplies on hand.

Before the party begins, on paper bags draw a Christmas stocking with a child's name on it. As the children make the ornaments they will take home, they can put them right into their own bag. This will minimize any confusion later on about whose ornament is whose.

When the children finish making the ornaments, you can serve the Christmas Tree Cake and hot chocolate. Ask the children to choose one of their ornaments to hang on your tree, and in just a few minutes your tree will shine with handmade treasures. Then gather everyone around the decorated tree to sing some of your favorite Christmas carols.

Christmas Tree Ornaments

Felt Christmas Ornaments Trace Christmas cookie cutter shapes like stars, bells, and angels onto felt; cut 2 of each shape. Bend a 2-inch piece of pipe cleaner into a hook. Sandwich the straight end of the pipe cleaner between the 2 felt pieces and glue them together. Glue sequins, bits of ribbons, and small buttons onto the felt.

Jeweled Ornaments Trace cookie cutter shapes onto the flat portion of aluminum foil food dishes and cut them out. With the point of the scissors, punch a small hole in the top of each one. Glue sequins onto both sides of the aluminum foil. Allow it to dry and attach a wire ornament holder through the hole.

Pomander Balls Push a thin skewer into the skin of a medium-size orange and insert a clove. Repeat all over the orange. Tie a ¼- or ⅜-inch-wide ribbon around the orange as shown and tie in a bow at the top. Insert a metal ornament holder into the bow. As the orange dries, it will add a lovely scent to the room.

Lollipop Angels Cut a 4-inch paper doily in half; fold one half in half for the skirt and cut the other half into quarters for the wings. Glue the skirt to the lollipop stick. Tape the wings together overlapping the points slightly, and glue them to the back of the lollipop stick. For the halo, make a circle at one end of a 6-inch pipe cleaner and bend the circle perpendicular to the pipe cleaner. Tape the straight end of the pipe cleaner to the back of the lollipop and the stick. For the angel's eyes and mouth, glue sequins onto the lollipop wrapper. Attach a wire ornament holder to the halo.

Three-Dimensional Stars Cut 2 stars from yellow posterboard. Make a cut in 1 from the bottom to the middle; make a cut in the other from the top to the middle. Slip the 2 together. Glue a loop of string to the top for hanging.

Foam Trees Cut a Christmas tree shape from the flat green foam that is used for packing fruit for shipping. Punch a hole through the top of the tree with the point of a pair of scissors or a large needle and thread a yarn loop through the hole. Decorate the tree with sequins or confetti and allow the glue to dry.

Paper Cup Bells Poke a hole in the bottom of a 3-ounce red or green paper cup, or one decorated with Christmas designs. To make the clapper, thread yarn through the hole in a large wooden bead. Knot one end; bring the other end from the inside of the paper cup through the hole, letting the bead dangle, and tie it in a bow. Attach an ornament holder through the yarn bow, and allow the glue to dry.

Christmas Tree Cake

What you need:
1 cake mix
1 can vanilla frosting
3 to 4 ounces coconut
Green food coloring
1 tube red decorating icing
2 tablespoons chocolate
  sprinkles
1½ ounces M&M's
¼ cup silver balls (optional)
Two 8-inch square cake pans
Cupcake pan
1 large star sticker or yellow
  construction paper
Wax paper

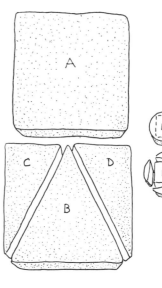

Make the cake following package directions and pour the batter into the 2 square pans and 2 cupcakes. When the cake is cool, level the layers and cut them following the diagram; arrange the pieces to form a tree. Level the cupcakes, trim them to squares, and place them at the bottom of the tree to form the trunk.

Color the coconut green, spread it out on a piece of wax paper, and allow it to dry. Add several drops of green food coloring to the frosting and frost the entire shape. Sprinkle the coconut on the tree. Put the chocolate sprinkles on the trunk and press them into the frosting. Draw a garland with red decorating icing. Add the candy and the silver balls. Place a star sticker on a piece of wax paper and cut around it. Or cut out a star from the yellow construction paper and glue it to a piece of wax paper. Place the star at the top of the tree.

HANUKKAH

*H*anukkah is called the Festival of Lights because it is celebrated by lighting candles for 8 nights. The special lamp is called a Hanukkah menorah and it has 8 candles. Hanukkah is a holiday full of cheer with games and gifts and songs; a great time for a party. Ask your guests to bring a wrapped gift for a grab bag. Cover a cardboard carton with blue and gold paper or with Hanukkah wrapping paper and have the guests place their gifts in the carton when they arrive. You'll want to have a dreidel and Hanukkah gelt, foil-covered chocolate coins, for each child. The children can make 3-Dimensional Dreidels and Noodle Menorahs, play several dreidel games, and choose a gift from the grab bag.

If your party is in the late afternoon, you can end by lighting the menorah candles and singing Hanukkah songs like "Rock of Ages," "The Dreidel Song," and "O Hanukkah."

For refreshments you can serve the traditional potato pancakes called latkes. Have both applesauce and sour cream and let the children decide which one they want on their pancakes. The Dreidel Cake can be the centerpiece of your party table.

3-Dimensional Dreidels

What you need:
Blue posterboard
Motifs cut from Hanukkah
    wrapping paper
String or yarn
Glue stick
Scissors

Cut 2 dreidel shapes out of posterboard for each child and make a
cut from the bottom to the center
on 1 and from the top to the center on the other. Have the
children decorate the 2 pieces by gluing motifs from wrapping paper on them. Put the dreidel together by sliding 1 piece
onto the other. Glue a loop of string or yarn to the top of the dreidel for hanging.

Noodle Menorah

What you need:
Lasagna noodles
Rigatoni noodles
White glue

Give each child 1 lasagna noodle and 10 rigatoni noodles. Have the children glue the tallest rigatoni noodle upright in the center of the lasagna
noodle for the shamash, then glue 4 more noodles on either side. Glue
the last noodle to the bottom of the lasagna noodle for a handle. Set aside
and allow the glue to dry.

Games

Hide the Dreidel Hide a dreidel in the room and have the children look
for it. As they get closer say "hotter" and as they move away from it say
"colder." When they have found the dreidel, give a dreidel to each child
so they can play the rest of the games.

Spin the Dreidel Give each player 10 pennies and put 10 pennies in a pot in the center. The symbol on the dreidel tells the child what to do. *Nun* is nothing: the child gets nothing. *Gimel* is all: the child takes all the pennies in the pot. *Hay* is half: the child takes half of the pot. *Shin* is put: the child puts 1 of his pennies into the pot. A child drops out if he loses all his pennies. The last player in the game wins.

The Longest Spin Have the children spin the dreidels to see who can keep the dreidel spinning the longest. No prizes are awarded for this; just encourage the children to continue practicing.

Pass the Dreidel The children sit in a circle and pass around a dreidel as music is played. When the music stops, the child holding the dreidel drops out. The last child remaining in the circle wins.

Pin the Shamash on the Menorah Make a menorah out of construction paper or posterboard, putting 8 candles on it, 4 on each side. Leave the center empty. Make separate shamash candles out of paper and put a piece of folded clear tape on the back of each. Blindfold each child in turn and see if they can pin the shamash in the center of the menorah.

Latkes

What you need:
4 to 5 large baking potatoes
3 eggs
3 tablespoons flour
1 teaspoon baking powder
Salt to taste
½ onion, grated (optional)
Oil for frying
Applesauce
Sour cream

Pare and coarsely grate the potatoes. Put the potatoes on several layers of paper towels to drain off the liquid. Mix the eggs, flour, baking powder, salt, and onion and add the potatoes. Fry 3 or 4 pancakes at a time in hot oil. To keep the cooked pancakes warm while you are making the others, place them on an aluminum foil–covered cookie sheet in a 200° F. oven.

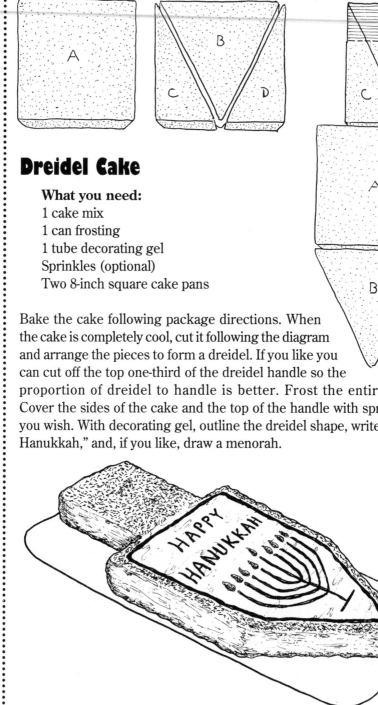

Dreidel Cake

What you need:
1 cake mix
1 can frosting
1 tube decorating gel
Sprinkles (optional)
Two 8-inch square cake pans

Bake the cake following package directions. When the cake is completely cool, cut it following the diagram and arrange the pieces to form a dreidel. If you like you can cut off the top one-third of the dreidel handle so the proportion of dreidel to handle is better. Frost the entire shape. Cover the sides of the cake and the top of the handle with sprinkles, if you wish. With decorating gel, outline the dreidel shape, write "Happy Hanukkah," and, if you like, draw a menorah.

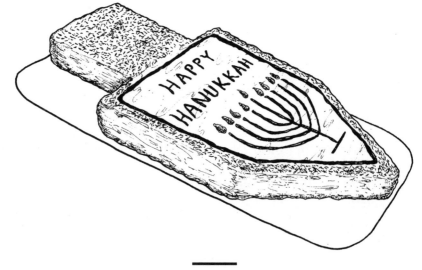

VALENTINE'S DAY

*V*alentine's Day is a time to celebrate the love all around us, the love of parents, of sisters and brothers, and of friends. Children can send Valentine's Day cards and sign their name, or surprise people by signing the card "from a secret admirer."

At this Valentine's Day party children can make cards, wreaths, puppets, and cookies all decorated with traditional symbols. While the children are working on their projects you can explain the meaning behind the symbols they use. Hearts have been a symbol of love since ancient times; ribbons are used because ladies gave ribbons to their favorite knights before they went off to war; roses are the flower of love; violets are, according to legend, the flower on which Saint Valentine wrote messages of love; and lace, from the Latin word meaning "to catch," is supposed to catch the heart of a loved one.

The night before the party you can make Valentine ice cubes. Place a frozen strawberry in each compartment of an ice cube tray. Fill the tray with a mixture of half orange juice and half water. When you serve the Heart Cake, add the Valentine ice cubes to lemonade or fruit punch.

Valentine's Day Cards

What you need:
Construction paper
Paper doilies
Scraps of fabric, ribbon, and yarn
Sequins
Metallic paper or aluminum foil
Pictures of flowers cut from seed
    catalogs
Crepe paper for ruffles
Glue
Clear tape
Scissors

Put all the supplies on the table along with scissors, glue, and clear tape. Also have heart-shaped cookie cutters and heart templates cut from cardboard to use as guides. Let the children make cards for their parents and friends.

Heart Wreath

What you need:
Cardboard, 9 inches square
Construction paper
Scraps of wrapping paper
   or wallpaper
Colored tissue paper
Glue stick and glue
Scissors

Cut out a 9-inch circle from the cardboard; cut out a 3-inch-wide circle from the center so you have a 3-inch-wide wreath. Cut the same size ring out of construction paper and glue them together. Cut out 2- to 3-inch hearts from the patterned wrapping paper or wallpaper. Crumple small pieces of colored tissue paper and glue them around the wreath. Glue a heart to the top of each piece of tissue paper.

Heart Puppet

What you need:
Empty paper towel tube
Construction paper
Yarn
12-inch pipe cleaners
Felt-tipped markers
Clear tape
Glue stick
Scissors

Cover the tube with construction paper, using 1 color for the top half of the tube and another color for the bottom half, and glue in place. Cut out a 5-inch heart from red construction paper. With markers and scraps of paper, make a face on the heart and clothes on the tube. Make a hat for the heart face. Cut pieces of yarn for straight hair or make loops for curly hair and glue to the back of the heart. Glue the heart to the tube. For arms, wrap a pipe cleaner around the middle of the tube and secure in the back with clear tape. Cut hands from paper and glue them to the pipe cleaner ends.

Heart Lollipop Cookies

What you need:
1 or 2 tubes refrigerated cookie dough
Heart-shaped cookie cutters
Several tubes cake decorating icing and decorating gel
Sprinkles and other cake decorations
Craft sticks
Several cookie sheets
Aluminum foil

Before the party begins, put the tubes of cookie dough in the freezer. When the guests arrive, preheat the oven according to package directions and line the cookie sheets with aluminum foil. Roll out the slightly hardened dough, cut out hearts with the cookie cutters, and place them on the cookie sheets. Carefully insert a craft stick into the bottom of each heart cookie. Bake as directed on the package. When the cookies have cooled slightly, decorate them with cake decorating icing and gel in a variety of colors. Add sprinkles and other decorations.

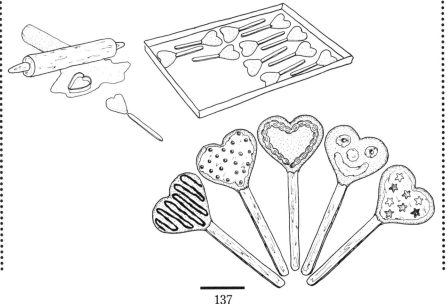

Heart Cake

What you need:
1 cake mix
1 can vanilla or cherry frosting
Red food coloring (optional)
1 tube red decorating gel
Candy hearts and sprinkles
Cake pans, one 8-inch square
 and one 8-inch round cake pan

According to package directions, make 1 square and 1 round cake. When they are cool, cut the round cake in half and arrange the pieces to form a heart. Make pink frosting by adding 1 or 2 drops of red food coloring to the vanilla frosting, or use cherry frosting. Frost the cake and decorate with candy hearts and sprinkles. With decorating gel write "We Love Our Friends" or "Happy Valentine's Day" on the cake.

EASTER

$\mathcal{E}$aster is a perfect time to have a party outdoors, but if the weather doesn't cooperate all of the games suggested here can be played inside. When the guests arrive, have them make their own Easter basket from a plastic fruit basket—the kind strawberries are sold in. The children can then move outside to play the Easter egg games. While the children are playing, you or a helper can fill the baskets with Easter grass, a decorated egg, and some candy so these favors will be ready for the children to take home at the end of the party.

When the children have finished playing the games, they can come back inside to a table set with the Easter Bunny Cake and Easter Basket Cupcakes. You can serve the cake and have the children take home a Basket Cupcake, or they may choose to eat their cupcake and leave the cake intact.

Easter Basket

What you need:
1 plastic pint-size strawberry basket
   for each child
Pastel-colored construction paper
Strip of lightweight cardboard,
   12 x ⅝-inches for each basket
Glue
Clear tape
Scissors

To make the basket handle, cut two 12 x ⅝-inch strips of construction paper in one of the colors you will be using in the basket. Glue them to the the front and back of the cardboard strip and set it aside while you weave the basket.

Measure the spaces between the horizontal ribs of the basket; it will be either ½ or ⅝ inch. Cut strips of construction paper to that width. You will need 2 strips each of 3 colors. Start weaving 1 paper strip through the bottommost spaces in the basket, going over and then under the plastic ribs. When 1 strip is used up, overlap the next strip, put a little glue on the overlapped area, and continue weaving. When you reach the beginning of the strip, overlap the ends, glue them, and cut off any excess paper. Weave the next color strip in the middle spaces, going over the ribs that the first color went under, and under the ribs the first color went over. Weave the third color strips through the top spaces. Bend the handle into a curve and tape the ends to the inside of the basket.

Games

Easter Egg Hunt Hide gaily decorated Easter eggs around the yard. Give each child a basket and ask them to find 2 or 3 eggs. It is a good idea to limit the number of eggs for each child so the younger children can have an equal chance with the older ones.

Egg Roll Line up hard-boiled eggs on the ground at the starting line. Give each child a large spoon. The child pushes the egg with the spoon. The first child to cross the finish line wins.

Egg Relay Race Divide the children into 2 teams. Give the first player a hard-boiled egg and a spoon. He walks fast to the finish line and back and hands the egg and spoon to the next player in line. If a player drops the egg he has to pick it up and continue walking. The first team to finish wins.

Pin the Ears on the Bunny On a white posterboard draw a bunny. Make separate ears out of white or pink construction paper and put a piece of folded clear tape on the back of each one. Blindfold each child in turn and see who can pin the ears on the bunny.

Bunny Rabbit Cake
& Easter Basket Cupcakes

What you need:
1 cake mix
1 can vanilla frosting
7 ounces coconut, divided
Green food coloring
3 gumdrops: 2 pink, 1 black
1 licorice shoelace
Jelly beans
One 8-inch round cake pan
Cupcake pans
Paper cupcake liners
Construction paper, 1 piece each white and pink
Toothpicks
Twelve 12-inch pipe cleaners
Scissors

Make the cake following package directions, making one 8-inch round layer and 12 cupcakes.

To make the Bunny Rabbit Cake, when the round layer is cool cut it in half. Place the halves upright and put frosting between them. Following the diagram, cut out a triangle to separate what will be the head and body; the triangle becomes the tail. Frost the entire shape, then cover it

with half the coconut. Cut the gumdrops in half horizontally and place the top rounded half into the frosting, pink for the eyes and black for the nose. For whiskers, cut four 1-inch pieces of licorice and push them into the cake next to the nose. Cut out 2 ears from the white and pink construction paper (see Out-of-the-Hat Cake, page 72). Attach the ears by inserting the toothpicks into the bunny's head.

To make the Easter Basket Cupcakes, frost all the cupcakes with the vanilla frosting. Add green food coloring to the remaining coconut. Put green coconut on top of each cupcake, then place 2 or 3 jelly beans in the center. To make a handle, fold a pipe cleaner in half. Twist the 2 halves around each other. Shape the twisted pipe cleaner into a curve and push the ends into the cupcake.

PASSOVER

*P*assover is a holiday that celebrates freedom and the start of a new life, and commemorates the Exodus of the Jewish people from Egypt. Passover comes in the spring when trees and plants are turning green and beginning a new life cycle.

Passover is often called the Festival of Unleavened Bread and is celebrated with a traditional family dinner called a Seder, at which guests are always welcome and children play an important role. Passover is a time to share. Because the Jewish people left Egypt in a hurry and didn't wait for their bread to rise, they cooked it on rocks in the hot sun. To commemorate this hard flat bread, we eat matzah. During the meal an adult breaks off a small piece of matzah and hides it. The children search for this matzah, called the afikoman, and when they find it they receive a small prize or coins.

At dinner the story of Passover is read aloud from a book called a Haggadah. The youngest child asks four questions, including "Why is this night different from all other nights?" and the answers are read from the Haggadah. Each person at the dinner has a copy of the Haggadah and before dinner begins, the children can make a cover for their copy. The children can also make a Seder Plate out of paper and draw the special foods that go on the plate. The games the children play are variations on traditional games, using nuts rather than balls or bean bags.

For dessert you can serve the Star of David Cake made with a special unleavened cake mix.

Haggadah Cover

What you need:
Construction paper
Felt-tipped markers
Stapler

Write the word "Haggadah" on a piece of construction paper and have the children color in the word and draw a picture or a design. Staple the cover to a plain piece of construction paper for the back cover. Slip each child's Haggadah inside the cover.

Seder Plate

What you need:
White paper plates
Scraps of construction paper
Felt-tipped markers
Glue stick
Scissors

Using the scraps of construction paper and the markers, the children can draw a border around the plate and create the special foods that go on the Seder plate: a bone that represents the lamb that was sacrificed; a hard-boiled egg and parsley to represent spring and rebirth; a bitter herb, usually horseradish, as a symbol of suffering; and haroset, a mixture of chopped apples, nuts, and wine, a symbol of the mortar with which the Jewish people used to build. Let the children glue the cutouts to the plate.

Games

Nut Toss Make a game board by taping together 6 paper cups, putting 3 in the bottom row, 2 in the center, and 1 at the top. Place this on the floor. The bottom 3 cups are worth 10 points, the center cups 20, and the top cup 30 points. Give each child 5 walnuts in the shell and see who can score the highest.

Pitching Nuts Place a box on the floor several feet from the children and give them walnuts to toss into the box. Move the box closer for younger children, farther away for the older ones. See who can get the most nuts into the box.

Almond in the Box Divide the children into 2 teams. The first player has a small box like a jewelry gift box, and the last player has an almond in the shell. The first player passes the box under his legs to the next player and who passes it under her legs and so on down the line. The last player puts the almond in the box and passes the box over her head to the player in front of her, who passes it over his head to the person in front of him and so on, until it reaches the front of the line. The first team to get the box back to the beginning wins.

Look for the Afikoman An adult hides half of the middle matzah during the Seder. After the dinner the children are told they may look for it. The one who finds it is rewarded with a prize, but usually small prizes or coins are given to all the children.

Star of David Cake

What you need:
Unleavened cake mix for a 2-layer cake
1 can frosting or homemade frosting
Chocolate spread or syrup
Two 8-inch round cake pans
Toothpicks

Make sure all ingredients are marked "Kosher for Passover." Bake the cake following package directions and allow it to cool.

Make a hexagon on 1 cake layer by measuring a line 3⅝ inches long and putting toothpicks at the end pints. Continue measuring this length line around the edge of the cake until you have 6 sides. Cut off the excess cake and remove the toothpicks.

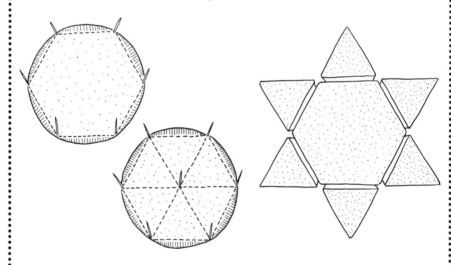

On the second layer, make a hexagon the same way, then mark the center of the cake. Connect these points to form 6 equal triangles. Cut the triangles, then cut away the excess cake. Remove the toothpicks. To form the Star of David, place the hexagon in the center of the plate and place a triangle so it extends from each side of the hexagon.

Set aside 3 tablespoons of frosting, then frost the cake. Add chocolate spread or syrup to the leftover frosting and put it in a small plastic bag (see page 21). With the chocolate frosting, outline the star and write "Happy Passover" on the cake.

MOTHER'S DAY

Mother's Day is a day set aside to honor Mom and one that children can make extra special by creating a party for their mother. The theme of this party is flowers and the children can make paper flowers to decorate the room, create a tissue paper flower bouquet to present to Mom, make a stand-up card of flowers, and transform a store-bought cake into a flower garden. Of course, the perfect way to start the day is to have the children, with some help in the kitchen, make breakfast for Mom and bring it to her on a tray.

A Stand-Up Card

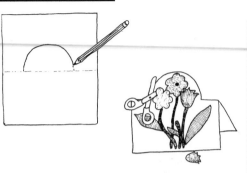

What you need:
Sturdy construction paper
Felt-tipped markers
Pencil
Glue or glue stick
Scissors

With the construction paper held vertically, mark the center of the paper. Draw a 5½-inch half-circle above the center line. Cut out 4 flowers about 1½ to 2 inches long, four 2-inch-long leaves, and four ¼-inch wide stems from construction paper. Glue these to the paper so that the top flowers fit inside the half-circle. Carefully cut out the half-circle that surrounds the flowers. Fold the card in half, being careful not to fold the flowers. Write "For Mom" on the outside of the card and write your message on the inside.

Flower Decorations

What you need:
Construction paper
Green pipe cleaners
Scissors
Hole punch

For the flower petals, cut 4-inch and 3½-inch circles from construction paper. Use 2 different colors or 2 different shades of 1 color. On the larger circle cut shallow petals around the edge. On the smaller circle cut deep petals, making them pointed or rounded or with fringed edges.

For the center of the flower, cut a 1½-inch circle in a contrasting color. With a hole punch, punch a hole in the center of each piece. (If you can't reach the center of the larger circle, punch a hole gently with the tip of the scissors.) Line up the layers and put 1 end of the pipe cleaner through the holes. Twist the pipe cleaner

146

end around itself to hold the paper layers. Cut free-form petals from green construction paper. Punch a hole at the base of a leaf and slip it on the free end of the pipe cleaner. Twist the pipe cleaner around the leaf hole to keep it in place. Do the same with each leaf.

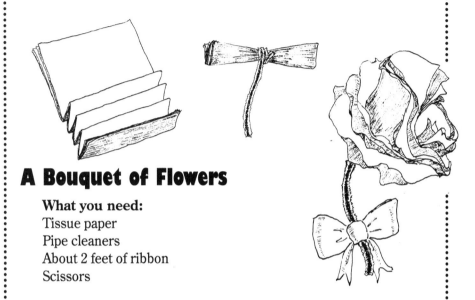

A Bouquet of Flowers

What you need:
Tissue paper
Pipe cleaners
About 2 feet of ribbon
Scissors

Cut four 8 x 12-inch pieces of tissue paper, mixing colors or using all one color. Holding the 4 pieces of paper together and starting at one short edge, accordion-fold them. Wrap a pipe cleaner around the center of the folded paper. Gently open up the folds on either side of the pipe cleaner stem so the flower is round, and separate the layers of paper slightly. Put several flowers together to make a bouquet and tie it with a ribbon bow.

A Flower Garden Cake

What you need:
1 frozen square cake
2 to 3 ounces coconut
Food coloring
Cake decorating gel
1 tube white decorating icing
1 package sugar wafer cookies
Butter cookies or vanilla wafers
Cake decorations and sprinkles
Craft sticks

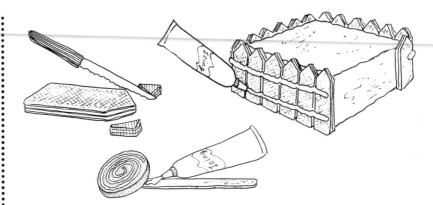

You can start with a frozen square or rectangular frosted cake right from the freezer for the flower garden. A 6- or 7-inch square cake uses 24 sugar wafers or 1 package. Cut 1 end of each sugar wafer into a point with a sharp knife and push them against the frosting on each side of the cake so they look like a picket fence. Make the fence rails by putting two lines of white decorating icing around the sugar wafer cookies.

Color the coconut green and set it aside. To make the flowers, apply decorating gel to the butter cookies and decorate them with sprinkles and cake decorations. Put a little decorating icing on 1 end of each craft stick and gently press a decorated cookie onto each one. Set these aside and allow the decorating icing to harden slightly.

Sprinkle the green coconut on the top of the cake. Insert the flowers by gently pushing the craft sticks into the top of the cake.

Tip

✔To make the craft sticks green so they look like flower stems, put several drops of green food coloring in a bowl and add several tablespoons of water. Use a cotton swab to paint the craft sticks with the food coloring. Allow the sticks to dry before you attach the cookies.

FATHER'S DAY

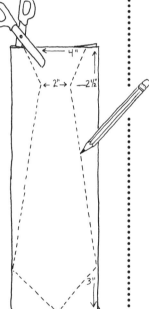

*F*ather's Day is the perfect time to surprise Dad with handmade gifts that will help him organize his day. Children can make a pad holder to hang near the telephone for taking notes and refrigerator magnets for keeping messages in easy view. They can start the day by making him a Father's Day Card in the shape of an oversized tie, and then make the biggest surprise of all, a Shirt and Tie Cake that looks just like Dad's shirt and tie.

Father's Day Card

What you need:
Construction paper,
　12 x 18 inches
Scraps of wrapping
　paper and stickers
6-inch piece of ribbon
Felt-tipped markers
Pencil
Hole punch
Scissors

Fold the construction paper in half lengthwise and draw a tie following the pattern shown. Cut out the 2 ties. On one tie create a design using markers, designs cut from wrapping paper, or stickers. On the second tie write your greetings with markers. Place the decorated tie on top of the second tie and punch 2 holes in the top of both. Cut the ribbon in half, thread the pieces through the holes, and tie the ribbons. If you do not want to use ribbon you can staple the ties together at the top.

149

Refrigerator Magnets

What you need:
Class photographs
Lightweight cardboard
Clip-type clothespins
1-inch-long magnets
Super glue
Scissors

To make a picture magnet, use a class photograph or any picture that is about 1 to 2 inches in size. Glue the photograph to lightweight cardboard and round the corners. Glue 2 magnets to the back of the cardboard.

To make a clip magnet, glue a magnet to the back of a clothespin. Allow the glue to dry. Children should be closely supervised when they are using Super glue.

A Pad Holder

What you need:
A small pad of paper
A piece of cardboard
   2 inches longer and wider
   than the pad
Construction paper
Buttons
6-inch length of yarn
White glue
Pencil
Ruler
Scissors
Craft knife
Stapler

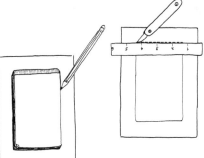

Cut the construction paper to the same size as the cardboard and glue it to the cardboard. Center the pad on the paper-covered cardboard and trace around it with a pencil. To make a slit in the cardboard to hold the pad, place a ruler along the top line of the pad outline and use a craft knife to cut through the cardboard. To hang the pad holder, make a loop with the yarn and staple the ends to the back of the cardboard.

Arrange your buttons by colors or size if you like. Place the buttons in the area around the outline of the pad. When you are pleased with the design, begin to glue each button in place. Allow the glue to dry, then slip the cardboard backing of the pad through the slit in the cardboard.

Shirt and Tie Cake

What you need:
1 square cake
2 tubes decorating gel
Sprinkles or colored sugar crystals
Toothpicks

> ### Tip
> ✔You could re-create your father's favorite tie on this cake by using the appropriate color decorating gel and choosing shapes from the many cake decorations available in the baking aisle of your supermarket.

You can use a purchased square cake, fresh or frozen, or make a square cake from a mix and frost it. On the top of the frosted cake use a toothpick to draw a man's tie in the center of the cake, starting with the knot at the top and then drawing the length of the tie. Draw the collar on either side of the knot and draw a pocket on the right side. With one color decorating gel, go over the lines of the tie, adding diagonal lines to make stripes. Fill in every other stripe with sprinkles or colored sugar crystals. With the second color decorating gel, go over the lines of the collar and pocket.

GRADUATION

*G*raduation from elementary or middle school is a wonderful occasion for a party. And to show your pride in the graduates, you can decorate the party room with excellent report cards for each guest. To make the report cards, on paper from a yellow-lined pad, write a child's name on top followed by "Report Card." Then list the subjects, either real subjects or ones you have made up like "Loves school," "Make friends easily," and "Likes parties." For some fun, you could write "Always on time" for the student who is often late, "Always prepared" for the student who usually forgets her books, and "Works quietly" for the most talkative student. But only do this if the children will think it is funny; you certainly do not want to hurt anyone's feelings. Give each student an A+ in every subject, add a gold star, and write "Promoted" on the bottom of the card.

This party consists entirely of games: some are games of skill, some require concentration, but all are fun to play. This is a time for the children to relax and enjoy themselves, to celebrate their success. Before you serve the refreshments, have the children give themselves a round of applause for a job well done. Then present the Diploma Cake.

Games

Puzzle Game On 9 x 12-inch sheets of construction paper write "Diploma" and add a gold sticker or draw a decoration. Cut each sheet in half in a different way. Give out a half diploma to each child as they arrive and ask them to find the child with the corresponding half.

Bowl for Prizes Have 1 small prize for each child and number the prizes. Have as many empty plastic soda bottles as you have guests, number them, and place them in a row. Give each child a chance to roll a foam ball into the pins and knock 1 down. The child wins the prize numbered the same as the bottle that was knocked down.

Stunts Before the party begins, write the letters in the name of your child's school on slips of paper with instructions for a stunt to be performed and put them in a bowl. To begin the game, assign each child a letter. Then let them choose a paper, find the person with the letter indicated on the paper, and ask that person to perform. At the same time the chooser will be sought out and asked to perform. Use letters only once even if they appear several times in the school's name. For the Bricktown School, you would use the letters B, R, I, C, K, T, O, W, N, S, H, and L. You could begin as follows:

B   Find S and ask that person to sing "Yankee Doodle."
R   Find H and ask that person to tell a joke.
I   Find L and ask that person to say something in French.
C   Find B and ask that person to hop around the room on 1 foot.
K   Find R and ask that person to recite the Pledge of Allegiance.
T   Find I and ask that person to do 3 sit-ups.

The result should be a room full of children singing, dancing, and reciting all at the same time.

Graduation Speech Write down 1-word subjects on separate pieces of paper and put them in a bowl. A child chooses a subject and gives a speech of 1 minute—use a kitchen timer—using her word as often as possible. For example, for the word "beach," a child might say, "A beach has lots of sand. I like going to the beach. The beach is hot. Ice cream melts at the beach. I like to eat hot dogs at the beach." You could award a prize to the child who uses his word the most.

Congratulations Graduate! This is a quiet game to play before you serve refreshments. Have the children write down as many words as they can find using the letters in the phrase "Congratulations Graduate."

Diploma Cake

What you need:
1 cake mix
1 can vanilla frosting
1 or 2 tubes decorating gel
1 tube decorating icing
1 foil-covered chocolate coin
Colored sugar crystals
Star-shaped cake decorations
9 x 13-inch cake pan
Dental floss
Toothpicks

Bake the cake following package directions. When it is cool, frost it completely. With dental floss held taut between your hands, make a line ½-inch from the edge of the top of the cake on all 4 sides. With a toothpick round off the corners. Go over the line with decorating icing. Place the chocolate coin in the bottom right corner. With decorating gel draw the outline of a ribbon at the bottom of the coin, and fill in with colored sugar crystals. With gel write "Congratulations Graduate" and the date, and decorate with stars.

FOURTH OF JULY

*F*ourth of July is a great time for a backyard barbecue and a day of old-fashioned fun and games. Set up a large table near the barbecue to hold the food, and cover it with a white paper tablecloth decorated with red, white, and blue crepe paper streamers and small American flags. Have the Flag Cake as the centerpiece of your buffet table. The menu is tried-and-true: hot dogs and hamburgers and all the trimmings.

For the activities you will want to have on hand marbles, jacks, sidewalk chalk, yo-yos, jump ropes, rubber balls, and a Hula-Hoop. Have the adults teach the children how to play with marbles, how to draw and play a game of Hopscotch, how to play Monkey in the Middle, and which jump rope rhymes they recited as a child. See who can keep the Hula-Hoop spinning the longest and who is most proficient at yo-yo tricks. As the sun sets, give each child a jar to catch fireflies.

Games

Balloon Volleyball Set up a net, divide the children into 2 teams, and play volleyball with a balloon. Blow up several balloons so you can replace the one in play when it breaks.

Flag Relay Race Designate a running track around the perimeter of your yard, if possible, or up and down a driveway. Divide the children into 2 teams. Give the first child in each team an American flag. The child runs around the track and hands the flag to the second child in line who then runs around the track carrying the flag and hands it to the next team member. The last player returns home. The first team to finish wins.

Dress-Up Relay Race Divide the children into 2 teams. For each team put a large T-shirt, a pair of shorts with an elastic waist (you could use men's boxer shorts), and a pair of rubber gloves at the goal line. Each child in turn runs to the clothes, puts on the rubber gloves and then puts on the shirt and shorts, takes off the shirt and shorts, removes the rubber gloves, and runs back to the line. The first team to finish wins.

Limbo Put a broom handle or other stick across the back of 2 chairs and have the children pass under the stick without touching it. Lower the stick to the inside rung of the chair, then to the chair seat, eliminating any child who touches the stick while passing under it. Keep lowering the stick. The child who can still fit underneath the stick at its lowest point is the winner.

Flag Cake

What you need:
1 cake mix
1 can vanilla
    frosting
1 pint strawberries
About 1 cup
    blueberries
9 x 13-inch cake pan

Bake the cake following the package directions. While the cake cools, wash and hull the strawberries and cut them into quarters, or sixths if they are very large, and wash the blueberries. Frost the cake. In the upper left corner of the cake mark off an area 5 x 3 ½ inches and fill it with blueberries placed in rows. Create the red stipes with rows of strawberry pieces; about 6 rows of strawberries will fit on the cake.

HALLOWEEN

No Halloween party would be complete without a scary playroom, a haunted hallway, or a ghostly garage. Choose an area of your house that won't be used for the party activities and set up a House of Horrors. When all of the guests have arrived, you or a teenage helper can lead the children through the area and then directly to the party room for the games.

After the games, take the children on a parade through the neighborhood to show off their costumes and to stop at a few houses to trick-or-treat. Take an instant photograph of each child in costume and put the photograph in the child's Trick-or-Treat bag at the end of the party. When the children return from their parade, serve the Jack-o'-Lantern Cupcakes and Witches' Brew, which is heated apple cider with a cinnamon stick stirrer.

The Haunted House Decorations

To decorate the walls, cut trees with spindly branches from brown wrapping paper. With black felt-tipped marker make the trees gnarled and full of knotholes. Attach the trees to the walls with tape.

Make hanging ghosts by covering an inflated balloon with a white plastic garbage bag. Tie a string under the balloon to make the head and draw facial features with a marker. Cut the bottom of the plastic bag into shreds. Hang the ghosts from the walls and ceiling.

Hang crepe paper streamers from the ceiling making them long enough so they will brush against the children's faces as they walk by. Cover the lights loosely with green crepe paper so the lights cast an eerie glow.

Buy cardboard skeletons and cobweb material and hang these from the trees. Put a jack-o'-lantern filled with dry ice on the floor. Add cornstalks, bales of hay, tree branches, or baskets of fall leaves. Scatter some leaves on the floor so the children will crunch on them as they walk through the room. Add any other decorations you have, such as a witch's hat and broomstick or a devil's pitchfork.

Buy a cassette tape of scary sounds (sold at variety stores with the Halloween decorations) and hide a tape recorder behind the decorations. Turn on the tape recorder right before the children start their scary walk.

Games

Bobbing for Apples Tie string around apples and hang them from a dowel or old mop handle so you can adjust the height for the children. Have 1 apple for each child and see who can grab the apple in with their teeth. If apples seem too difficult, try hanging bagels for the children to bite.

Fish for Spiders Attach a paper clip to plastic spiders and bugs and put them in a tub of water. Make a fishing rod by attaching a magnet to a string and tying the string to a pole. Have enough spiders and bugs so the children can fish for several of them.

Peanut Toss Cover a cardboard carton with orange crepe paper and draw a jack-o'-lantern face on it with black marker. Give each child 4 or 5 peanuts and have them stand several feet from the box. See how many peanuts they can toss into the box.

Bean the Ghost Cover a large carton with white paper or paint it white. Cut out eyes, nose, and mouth, making the holes large enough for a bean bag to fit through easily. Give each child 3 bean bags to throw through the holes.

Scary Story This is a great game for a teenage helper to run. Before the party begins, get together the props: a rubber glove stuffed with old pantyhose for a hand, cold cooked spaghetti for the intestines, peeled grapes for the eyeballs, cut-up pieces of licorice shoelace for toenails, potato chips for scabs, dried apricots for ears, pudding in a plastic bag for the heart, and any other equally tasteless items that children will love. Go to your library to find a scary story or poem for Halloween, or make one up. Have the children sit in a circle on the floor, turn off the lights, and tell the story in a scary voice as you pass around the appropriate props.

Jack-o'-Lantern Cupcakes

What you need:
1 cake mix
1 can vanilla frosting
Food coloring
1 tube green decorating gel
12 to 15 green gumdrops
2 licorice shoelaces
Cupcake pans
Tweezers

Follow package directions make 24 to 30 cupcakes, filling each one less than half full. Let them cool. Level the tops with a serrated knife. You will be putting 1 cupcake on top of another with the leveled tops together. You can make 12 to 15 jack-o'-lanterns with 24 to 30 cupcakes.

Make orange frosting by adding red and yellow food coloring to the vanilla frosting. Put some frosting between the cupcakes, put them together, and frost them completely. Cut a gumdrop in half and put the rounded half on top of the cupcake for a stem. Draw leaves with green decorating gel. Cut the licorice into ½- and ¼-inch pieces and, using tweezers, arrange the pieces to form the jack-o'-lantern's features.

Tip

✔When making colored frosting, even bright orange for these pumpkin faces, always begin by adding only 1 or 2 drops of each color. Gradually add more food coloring to make the frosting a darker or brighter.

THANKSGIVING

*T*hanksgiving is a holiday where all generations of a family gather together to give thanks for and to share what they have. The job of putting a dinner on the table can be shared by all the guests and it can even become a game. Before the guests arrive, write down on slips of paper as many jobs as there are guests. Write down easy jobs such as getting the butter out and putting the napkins on the table for the younger children, as well as difficult ones like carving the turkey and putting the food on the table for the adults. Put the slips of paper in a bowl in the foyer. As guests arrive ask each person to choose a piece of paper and to take care of that particular job.

Also in the foyer hang a poster that says "What We Are Thankful For" and put a pad of self-stick pages and a pen near it. As guests arrive, ask each person to write down what they are thankful for: material things, successes of the past year and other intangible things, and people they care for. Have the guests stick their notes on the poster. When the family is ready to sit down at the table, have several people read the notes to help evoke the feeling of thankfulness and the reason for this big dinner.

As dinner is being prepared, ask the children to make place mats, place cards, and a table runner for the dinner table, and to fold napkins into a shape that looks like turkey feathers.

Place Mats

What you need:
12 x 18-inch construction paper
Leaves
Crayons

Put the leaves on a table or work surface in any pattern and place a piece of construction paper on top of them. With the side of a crayon, rub the paper until the veins and outline of the leaf are visible. Use different color crayons for each leaf or use the same color; use the same shape leaf or a variety of leaves. Each place mat can be different.

Table Runner

What you need:
Construction paper, 9 x 12 or 12 x 18 inches
Leaves
1 or 2 rolls crepe paper streamers (optional)
Crayons

If you are using 9 x 12-inch paper, cut each piece in half horizontally. If you are using the larger paper, cut in half vertically. With crayons, rub over the leaves as described for the place mats. Then tape the 6-inch-wide papers together until you have a piece as long as the length of your dining room table. Place the runner on the table and if you wish, tape crepe paper streamers along either side of it, letting the ends of the streamers hang over the edges of the table.

Place Cards

What you need:
3 x 5-inch unlined colored
   index cards
Animal crackers
White glue
Felt-tipped markers

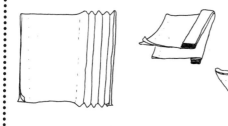

Fold the cards in half lengthwise. Glue an animal cracker to the left side of the folded card and write a person's name in the remaining space. If you think young children may want to eat the animal cracker, use a dab of decorating icing to secure it rather than glue.

Turkey Feathers Folded Napkins

Use a 17-inch square or larger paper or cloth napkin. Fold the napkin in half. If you're using a paper napkin that comes folded in quarters, open it up so that it is folded in half only. Fold the napkin into

1-inch accordion pleats, leaving the last 3 or 4 inches unfolded. Fold this in half with the pleats on the outside. Fold up the bottom left corner and tuck it into the pleats. Stand the napkin up so the pleats form a fan.

Turkey Cake

What you need:
1 cake mix
1 can milk chocolate frosting
4 ounces coconut
Food coloring
1 tube white decorating icing
1 licorice twist
12 red hots
2 pieces candy corn
One 9-inch round cake pan
Cupcake pans

Mix the cake following package directions. Bake the cake in one 9-inch round cake pan and make 14 cupcakes. While the cake is cooling, color the coconut. Divide the coconut into thirds and tint one-third yellow, one-third orange, and one-third red.

To make the turkey's head, cut the rounded top and ¼ inch of the most rounded cupcake. From the bottom of the cupcake cut a triangle for the beak. From another cupcake cut 2 rectangles for the neck.

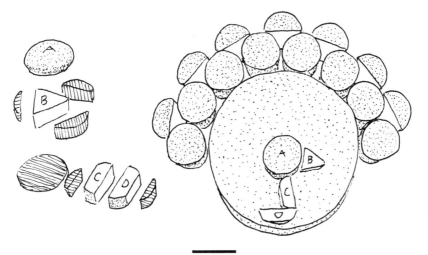

Place the round cake in the center of a tray and frost the top and sides. Frost the tops of 8 cupcakes and place them around the top of the cake. Frost the sides of the cupcakes. Cut 4 cupcakes in half. Put 7 half-cupcakes around the original 8, placing them where 2 whole cupcakes meet. Frost the tops and outer rounded sides of these half-cupcakes. (Don't worry about getting frosting between all the cupcakes because they will be covered with coconut.)

Frost the cupcake for the turkey's head and place it in the center of the cake, about two-thirds of the way down from the top. Frost the beak and neck pieces and place them on the cake. Dip a butter knife into water and smooth the frosting on the head, beak, and neck. Place 6 red hots in 2 groups of 3 on top of the head for the crown and place 5 red hots under the beak for the wattle. Place 2 pieces of candy corn on the beak. Put a dot of white decorating icing on the head for the eye and place a very small red hot in the center of the white icing.

Sprinkle the red coconut on the half-cupcakes, the orange coconut on the whole cupcakes, and the yellow coconut on the upper edge of the cake. Use all of the coconut to give fullness to the feathers and do not leave any spaces between the coconut colors. Cut two 2-inch pieces of licorice twist for the feet. To make the 3 toes, on the bottom of each piece make 2 cuts ¾ inch long and separate the 3 pieces of licorice slightly. With a knife make 2 slits in the bottom of the cake and insert the licorice feet into the cake.

NEW YEAR'S EVE

Stage a Masked Ball for New Year's Eve and invite the children to come dressed in costume. At the party the children can make masks on a stick to add to their costume and New Year's noisemakers, then play games until the countdown to midnight (or a prearranged time that you will designate as midnight if the party is to end earlier). At the bewitching hour the children can put on their masks and ring in the New Year with their noisemakers. To toast the New Year, serve ginger ale in plastic champagne glasses, and end the celebration with the Party Hat Cake.

The Masks

What you need:
Lightweight cardboard
Drinking straws
Curling ribbon
Feathers
Fabric and paper scraps
Glitter
Felt-tipped markers
Glue
Clear tape
Scissors

Draw a mask shape that is about 6 inches wide on cardboard and cut it out. Color the mask with markers and add glitter, curled ribbon, a feather, or fabric or paper scraps. Tape a straw to the mask for the stick.

New Year's Noisemakers

What you need:
5- or 7-ounce plastic drinking cups
¼ cup uncooked rice
Cloth tape to match cups
Permanent felt-tipped markers

Have the children draw designs on 2 cups with the markers. Put a scant ¼ cup of rice in one cup. Upend the second cup on top of it and hold the 2 together by wrapping cloth tape around them twice.

Games

Musical Months Countdown This game is played like Musical Chairs, using pieces of paper on the floor rather than chairs. On separate pieces of construction paper write the names of the months and one for the New Year and place them on the floor. Play music. When the music stops, anyone not standing on a paper is out. Remove one paper each round, starting with January and ending with the New Year.

Sing for Your Supper Play this game with the entire group. See if the children can come up with a song that is appropriate for each month of the year and sing a few lines of the song. The song can have the name of the month in it, be about a holiday in that month, or have an appropriate topic such as snow in January or swimming in July.

Resolutions Have the children write down 1 or more resolutions, funny or serious, for the New Year. Mix up the papers and give 1 to each child to read. See if the group can identify the writer.

Party Hat Cake

What you need:
1 cake mix
1 can frosting
2 ounces coconut or ¼ cup sprinkles
1 tube decorating gel
Star-shaped cake decorations
9 x 13-inch cake pan
Cupcake pan

Mix the cake following package directions; make one 9 x 13-inch cake and 4 cupcakes. When the cake is cool, cut a triangle from the top center to the bottom corners as shown. For the bottom layer of the hat put the 2 smaller triangles together and trim the bottom straight across. Frost the top of this layer and then place the large triangle on top of it.

For the pompom, level 1 cupcake and frost it. Put another cupcake on top of it and place the 2 of them at the top of the triangle. Level the

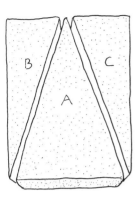
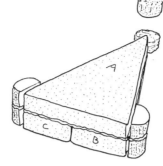

remaining 2 cupcakes. Put frosting on 1 cupcake, place the second one on top of it, and cut them in half. Place each half on either side of the bottom of the hat. Frost the entire shape. Put tinted coconut or sprinkles on the pompon and along the bottom 2 inches of the hat. With decorating gel write "Happy New Year" on the cake and sprinkle it with star-shaped cake decorations.

BABY'S CHRISTENING

*a*t a party in honor of a new baby's christening the guests will probably range in age all the way from infant relatives and friends to the baby's grandparents. To keep the young kids busy while the grown-ups coo over the baby, you can have them decorate undershirts for the baby. This crafts project will give the children something to do and will result in a wardrobe of fanciful shirts for the baby. While you set up a buffet lunch, ask the teenagers in the group to play some relatively quiet games with the children. The Baby Carriage Cake can be the centerpiece of the luncheon table.

Decorated Undershirts

What you need:
White or pastel baby undershirts
Stencils
Felt-tipped fabric markers
Shirt cardboards
Masking tape

Place a piece of cardboard between the front and back of the baby undershirts. Give the children some simple stencils like hearts, stars, toys, and the alphabet. Help the children place the stencil and tape it to the shirt with masking tape. To make a design on the shirt, the children fill in the open areas of the stencil with fabric markers. With the alphabet stencils they can spell out the baby's name or initials. The fabric markers will dry very quickly, but follow the marker package instructions for handling the shirts.

Games

Sweet Baby Write out the baby's full name—first, middle, and last—and ask the children to think of an adjective that begins with each letter.

Visiting Baby Matthew The children sit in a circle on the floor and say, "I went to visit baby Matthew and I brought *a blanket.*" The object a child brings must begin with the same letter as their first name. The leader says, "Yes you may go" or, "No you may not go." To help them, say Jessica cannot bring candy but she can bring jelly beans.

Crying Baby This is a version of Hot Potato. The children sit in a circle and pass around a baby doll as music plays. When the music stops, the child holding the crying baby is out. The child left holding the baby at the end of the game can be awarded a prize.

Baby Search Hide baby items around the room but in full sight. Give each child a piece of paper and a pencil and have them write down the items as they see them without touching the items or telling anyone what they saw. You could hide a rattle, a block, a diaper pin, a baby comb, a container of baby powder, booties, a bib. The child with the highest number of items after 5 minutes of searching wins.

Animal Babies Make a list of animals and another of the names of animal babies and see if the children can match the animal name with its offspring. You can use dog and puppy, cat and kitten, cow and calf, horse and foal, bear and cub, deer and fawn, goose and gosling, owl and owlet. For older children you may want to include more difficult animals such as penguin and chick, spider and spiderling, buffalo and calf, kangaroo and joey.

Baby Carriage Cake

What you need:
1 cake mix
1 can frosting
1 tube decorating gel
One 8-inch round cake pan
Cupcake pans

Mix the cake following package directions and bake one 8-inch round layer and 12 cupcakes. You will need 2 cupcakes for the carriage wheels; the remaining 10 can be decorated with the baby's initials or birth date.

When the cake is cool, cut a 3-inch-wide wedge from the cake and remove it. Place the 2 cupcakes below the round layer. Frost the entire shape. With decorating gel outline the carriage shape and add radiating lines for the carriage hood. Draw the wheels and spokes. Write the baby's name and birth date on the body of the carriage.

CONFIRMATION

a party for a Confirmation or First Communion is a lovely way to celebrate a child's affirmation of faith and coming of age in the eyes of the Church. If the party will include friends and relatives of different ages, you can play some games, such as the Famous Pairs game and the Songfest described below, that will be fun for both children and adults to play together. You can also plan some games that are for the children only and award prizes to the players.

If you plan to serve a buffet lunch, decorate the table with blue and white crepe paper streamers and have the Cross Cake as the table centerpiece. To pay tribute to the guest of honor ask each adult and child to share something special about the honored guest, to tell his favorite characteristic of, or fondest experience with that person.

Games

Famous Pairs Write down the names of famous pairs from the Bible such as Adam and Eve, David and Goliath, Moses and Aaron, Mary and Joseph, separately on self-sticking labels. Give 1 to each guest as they arrive and ask them to find the person who has the other half of the pair.

Sit On It Write the names of biblical characters on small slips of paper, put them inside balloons, and blow up the balloons. Put the names of characters from one Bible story on a piece of paper and hang it on the wall. Have the children sit on the balloons to break them. If the name in their balloon matches a name on the wall, they win a prize. If you want everyone to win a prize, write each set of biblical characters on separate pieces of paper and have different small prizes for each set of characters.

Songfest On separate pieces of paper write 1-word subjects such as love, grace, and the Cross, about which many hymns have been written. Fold the papers and put them in a bowl. Divide the guests into 2 or more teams. Have each team choose a topic and give them 2 minutes to sing a hymn based on the topic they chose.

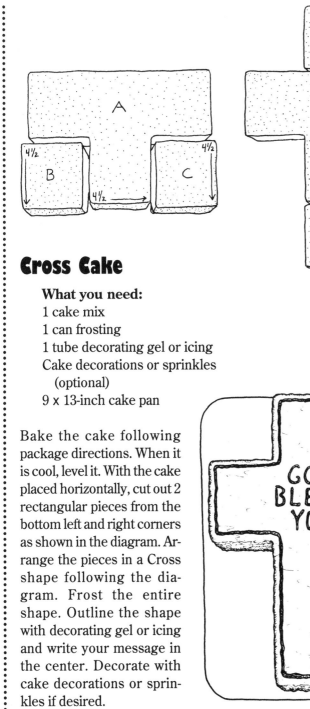

Cross Cake

What you need:
1 cake mix
1 can frosting
1 tube decorating gel or icing
Cake decorations or sprinkles
(optional)
9 x 13-inch cake pan

Bake the cake following package directions. When it is cool, level it. With the cake placed horizontally, cut out 2 rectangular pieces from the bottom left and right corners as shown in the diagram. Arrange the pieces in a Cross shape following the diagram. Frost the entire shape. Outline the shape with decorating gel or icing and write your message in the center. Decorate with cake decorations or sprinkles if desired.

BABY'S FIRST BIRTHDAY

*B*aby's first birthday is a time for the parents to celebrate that wonderful first year of life. Although a first birthday party usually includes friends with small children, the party is not a traditional children's party. To help the young children feel a part of the celebration, you can ask them to bring as a gift a copy of one of their favorite storybooks. The children will feel important because they chose their own gift for the birthday child, and the birthday child will receive a small library of classic children's stories.

At the party the children can make the birthday child a banner and then display it in the party room. An adult or a teenager can play some games with the children before the refreshments are served. Everyone will love the Baby Blocks Cake.

Birthday Banner

What you need:
Construction paper
Felt-tipped markers
Hole punch
Hole reinforcements
5 yards yarn or narrow ribbon

Decide what you want the banner to say: "Happy Birthday Kevin" or "Kevin is 1 year old" or your own message. Give out the construction paper and ask the children to hold the paper vertically and make 1 big letter that covers the entire page on each piece of paper. The children can decorate the letter with designs made with felt-tipped markers. Punch 2 holes in the top of each page and glue on reinforcements. Thread the yarn or ribbon through the holes, leaving a space between the words. Make sure the letters are in the correct order as you thread them. Then hang the banner for all the guests to see.

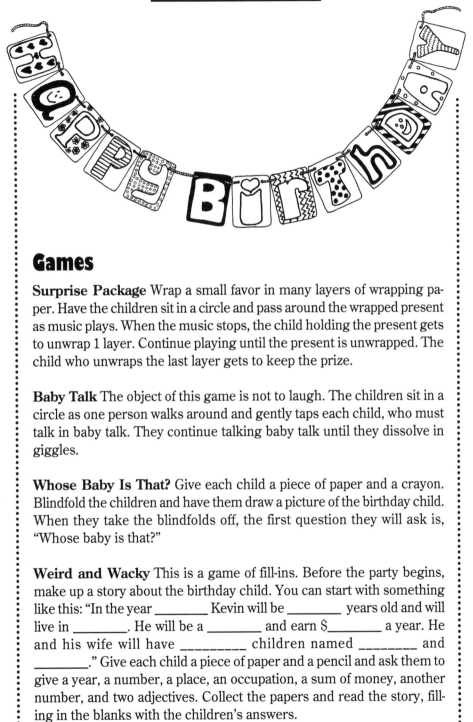

Games

Surprise Package Wrap a small favor in many layers of wrapping paper. Have the children sit in a circle and pass around the wrapped present as music plays. When the music stops, the child holding the present gets to unwrap 1 layer. Continue playing until the present is unwrapped. The child who unwraps the last layer gets to keep the prize.

Baby Talk The object of this game is not to laugh. The children sit in a circle as one person walks around and gently taps each child, who must talk in baby talk. They continue talking baby talk until they dissolve in giggles.

Whose Baby Is That? Give each child a piece of paper and a crayon. Blindfold the children and have them draw a picture of the birthday child. When they take the blindfolds off, the first question they will ask is, "Whose baby is that?"

Weird and Wacky This is a game of fill-ins. Before the party begins, make up a story about the birthday child. You can start with something like this: "In the year _____ Kevin will be _____ years old and will live in _____. He will be a _____ and earn $_____ a year. He and his wife will have _____ children named _____ and _____." Give each child a piece of paper and a pencil and ask them to give a year, a number, a place, an occupation, a sum of money, another number, and two adjectives. Collect the papers and read the story, filling in the blanks with the children's answers.

Baby Blocks Cake

What you need:
1 cake mix
1 can frosting
¼ cup jam or jelly
1 tube decorating icing
1 or more tubes decorating gel
Two 8-inch square cake pans

Bake the cake following package directions. When the cake is cool, level the tops and spread jelly on top of 1 layer. Place the second layer on top of it. Cut the cake into quarters. You will have four 2-layer squares. Frost each square completely. With decorating icing outline all 12 edges of each square. With decorating gel write A, B, C, and D on the front of the blocks and write your message on the top.

> **Tip**
> ✔If you spread jam or jelly between the layers of any 2-layer cake, you will have more frosting for the outside of the cake.

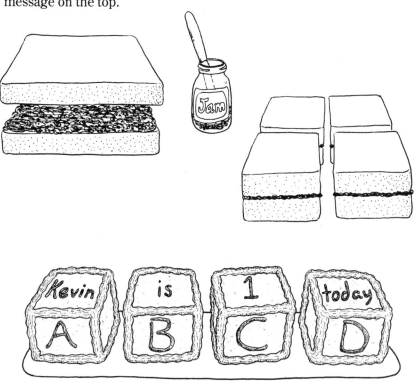

INDEX

Conversion Chart

Solid Measures			Linear and Area Measures	
U.S. and Imperial Measures		Metric Measures	1 inch	2.54 centimeters
ounces	pounds	grams	1 foot	0.3048 meters
1		28		
2		56		
3 ½		100		
4	¼	112		